Experiential Lea

Norman Evans

CASSELL

Cassell
Villiers House
41/47 Strand
London WC2N 5JE

387 Park Avenue South
New York
NY 10016-8810

First published 1994

British Library Cataloguing-in-Publication Data
A catalogue record for this book is available from the British Library.

ISBN: 0-304-33100-7 (hardback)
 0-304-33102-3 (paperback)

Typeset by Action Typesetting Limited, Gloucester
Printed and bound in Great Britain by Biddles Ltd, Guildford and King's Lynn

Contents

Preface

Since 1979, when I began working to encourage developments in experiential learning and its assessment in Britain, the topic has moved from the periphery of debate about education and training to its very centre. There is nothing surprising in that. It was a concept whose time had come, for economic, demographic and societal reasons. Consequently experiential learning has become an issue for many educational institutions, employing bodies and, indeed, for government too.

This book offers a snapshot identification of experiential learning in the various contexts in which it has developed over the last decade. Each chapter provides a different focus and, in doing so, draws on the experience of friends and colleagues in higher education, adult education, employment, and those who have worked on other projects. Without the benefit of their experience the book could not have been written. No doubt they will disagree with some of the arguments I have put forward; where they hold me wrong I shall hope to go on learning experientially from them.

In particular I have valued and benefited greatly from the collaborative work with my colleagues at the Learning from Experience Trust: Michèle Bailleux, Jeff Braham, Gerald Dearden, Corrine Henebery, John Storan, John Taylor and Anthony Turner. They have given me much good counsel. Similarly I am grateful for critical though supportive comments from Martin Johnson at the Further Education Unit, Mike Field, Principal of Croydon College, and from many of the adult educators I met during the early days of UDACE, all of whom taught me a great deal about experiential learning in their fields. Since 1986, when he joined the Employment Department as a Senior Professional Adviser at the Training, Enterprise and Education Directorate of the Employment Department, David Pierce has kept in touch with the work of the Trust, an association which has been consistently stimulating.

My largest debt of all is to Morris Keeton, the founding President of CAEL, whose every conversation sparks off some new idea, some new way of looking at things and to other American friends for deepening my explorations and expanding understandings.

I hope that anyone who has a general interest in experiential learning or who thinks that it may offer scope for developing their work, whether in education, employment or policy development, may find something useful in these pages.

Norman Evans
July 1994

1

APEL: What Is It?

'Experiential learning means the knowledge and skills acquired through life and work experience and study which are not formally attested through any educational or professional certification' (FEU, 1983). I wrote that in 1983 and as a working definition it seems to hold good. Hence the assessment of prior experiential learning (APEL) refers to all learning which has not been assessed. This marks it off from the assessment of prior learning (APL), which also includes learning which has been assessed for some formal purpose. Thus APEL is a sub-set of APL. There is considerable discussion about APL these days in many quarters, so it is as well to clarify the difference.

In some ways the labels are very pedantic in that all learning is prior, that is achieved before it can be assessed. But in specialist usage, 'prior' learning now refers to all the learning which has been acquired and which is being presented for assessment for some new purpose, which could be seeking a qualification, entry to a course of study, or credit towards a course or qualification. Some of that learning could have been acquired through a formal process, which may have led to a qualification; and some of it may be experiential. The difference between the two is that whereas prior learning has some kind of formal record, prior experiential learning has none, for the simple reason that by definition it has been acquired from experience and has not been documented. The discussion in this book is about experiential learning. Although there are overlapping areas the distinction is important.

In one sense experiential learning ought not to be an issue at all. It is as valid a way of learning as learning from books, lectures or laboratories. Learning either is or is not learning, so as a learning mode, experiential learning is just one mode among many others. So why is it now an 'issue'?

The steady development of formal education since the nineteenth century resulted in a mistaken view that significant learning is that which takes place in formal institutions and, in particular, leads to examination results, certificates and qualifications. But as formal education in schools – which was rigid, characterized by rote learning and endless repetition of mechanical tasks – came to seem ineffective, worrying pedagogical questions arose. If the justification for spending public money on universal schooling was to produce an educated people who as responsible citizens could play their part politically in a democracy as well as contributing economically to their country, then how could they be helped to learn more effectively? It was this line of thought which led John Dewey in particular to assert that learning by doing was a necessary complement to more abstract forms of learning. And from then onwards a controversy has continued about teaching methods and the curriculum generally. In 1967 the Plowden Report, *Children and their Primary Schools*, gave powerful support for the Dewey approach. The Newsom Report, *Half our Future*, had done the same for secondary schools in 1963. However, some, though by no means all, of the education reforms since 1979 have represented a reversion to a more formal approach to learning in schools. By contrast, in further and higher education, the interest in different forms of students' learning and in student-centred study has increased in recent years, making Dewey and the many subsequent developments of his work powerful contemporary influences. In this context experiential learning has become important because, with its assumption that informally acquired knowledge and skill may be as significant as learning through any formal means, it represents the recognition that individuals can and do learn by doing as well as through formal instruction, and most important, that many learn without being taught at all.

As a proposition, experiential learning is disarmingly simple; yet it is highly controversial. It is simple because there is nothing more obvious than saying that people learn from experience. Or may do so. Of course there is nothing inevitable about learning from experience. Everyone can think of people who have long experience and appear to have learned nothing from it. Leave that on one side and the simplicity remains; experience can be a source of learning. It is controversial because it challenges directly so many well-established ways of doing things in education and, as a matter of fact, in employment as well.

This is what makes experiential learning so important: part of its significance lies at the point where the activities in the world of formal education and the work-a-day world of employment meet. They meet in the ever more urgent question of the employability of people, men and women, young, middle-aged and old, of all ethnic backgrounds. Whether in connection with younger people entering employment for the first time, those who have experience of employment and need to keep their knowledge and skills up to date, or the unemployed facing all the problems of either entering employment for the first time or re-entering employment, experiential learning increasingly comes into the reckoning. And that raises questions for both education and employment.

Another part of its significance lies in the contribution it can make to fulfilling government policies of increasing the participation rates in all forms of post-secondary education. This increase necessarily means including greater numbers of students from those sections of the population which do not participate at present. It also means expanding the range and type of learning opportunities on offer. Experiential learning has a good deal to offer to both implications of these policies.

So for education and vocational training, employment and individuals, experiential learning is a national issue connecting with the policies of government, with employing organizations and with teaching institutions and will run strongly throughout the 1990s and beyond.

At the same time experiential learning can have different meanings for different people. Everyone tends to bring their personal predilections and interests to any topic, and so it is with this one: put any group of people in the same room to talk about experiential learning and different emphases are almost certain to emerge.

There are those who set great store on the power of experiential learning to promote the growth and development of individuals. They claim its psychological value for individuals who undervalue themselves, and whose confidence is boosted by realizing how much they have learned and can continue to learn from experience.

Some take that argument further: they say that the empowering of individuals implied by that contribution to growth and development can have profound consequences for the role they play in society. With greater self-confidence in their capacity as learners, the way they think and act politically, economically and personally can enable them to take greater control over their lives. For those who put this emphasis on experiential learning, it offers a way of trying to change society.

Another group concentrates their interest on experiential learning as a teaching technique. As experienced teachers they claim, like Dewey, that there are many people who learn effectively through doing things, and having learned that way successfully, are subsequently better able to learn in more abstract ways from books and formal instruction. So they interpret experiential learning as referring to practical activities of all kinds, to field work, whether programmes like Outward Bound, leadership and management training, observation and interview work or simulations and group work. This is the practice into theory argument.

Then there are those whose particular concern for experiential learning lies in its assessment and accreditation. They assert that it is critical for individuals to get due recognition for whatever knowledge and skill they have acquired, irrespective of how they acquired it, and that it is part of the responsibility of educational institutions to ensure that an assessment and accreditation service exists.

Some go further: they point to the implications for institutions of providing that service. Introducing the new assessment/accreditation system will necessitate a review of admission, assessment and examination procedures, advice and counselling facilities, teaching methods and the curriculum, as well as ways of financing those activities. Thus they see experiential learning as a way of helping to change institutions and equip them to do their job properly in the circumstances in which they now find themselves.

For many staff in institutions, however, the theory and practice of experiential learning has an intellectual appeal. It raises epistemological questions about knowledge and the validity of the ways disciplines are organized and managed. For others experiential learning offers a way of putting into practice their sense of vocation in the true sense of the word, because they hold that policies for greater participation rates raise ethical questions relating to social justice. For them, giving recognition to accomplishments irrespective of how they were achieved is part of their contemporary professional responsibility as well as a task for education.

Allied to this is the value of experiential learning for individuals whose experience of formal education has discouraged them from continuing to learn in any formal sense, who often have little confidence in their ability to learn in a formal setting and are diffident, even reluctant, to approach institutions in the formal system.

But as with any human activity, in any group apparently sharing the same interest there are as many interpretations of that interest as there are members in the group. This is as true of experiential learning as any other topic. So running across and through those broad groups of interest in experiential learning there will tend to be those who are fully committed to the enterprise, those who are quite willing to go along with what looks like an interesting development, those who simply go along for the ride, and the odd maverick who chases anything which sounds and looks like being radical. And of course, again as with all human groups, motives are always compounded of professional and private interests. So as an issue for individuals, experiential learning can have many flavours.

This is the case not only in Great Britain. The Americans led the field in the recognition and assessment of experiential learning from the early 1970s. At the end of that decade the story of development began to unfold in Britain. During the 1980s interest began to quicken in France, Canada and Australia, in the last two years New Zealand and in 1994, South Africa. There is now active interest in Indonesia and it could well be that applications of experiential learning develop in other developing countries and in Eastern Europe.

With such a wide range of interpretations of the prime potential benefits to be had from experiential learning, and given the different countries in which these interests are developing, it is obvious that there are overlapping preoccupations: interest in individuals cannot be neatly separated from what an institution provides for them, and how it provides it. Pedagogical interest in experiential learning cannot ignore questions of assessment and accreditation. And someone who takes a political view of the role of education in society is likely to want experiential learning to be a catalyst for change all round. It is hardly surprising, therefore, that experiential learning is a hot contemporary topic. The speed with which the very words experiential learning have spread though discourse on education and training indicates as much.

REFERENCES

Evans, Norman (1983): *Curriculum Opportunity*. London: FEU.
Newsom Report (1963) London: HMSO.
Plowden Report (1967) London: HMSO.

2

APEL and Individuals

These days any individual, any family, any street, any club or voluntary organization, any place of employment, can present an amazing array of experiences. People live in different ways: urban, rural, in house or flat; they shop at supermarkets or local shops, do or do not have children who may or may not be in school; walk, cycle, bus, drive, commute to work; are single parents, childless, partners, single, married households. People work in offices, shops, factories, all forms of public services – transport, medical, education, social services – or drive around most of the day as salesmen, work on farms or in the hugely expanded leisure industry. Most people have a number of leisure activities. They sail, walk, ramble, mountaineer, go caving, visit historic houses, places and gardens. They go abroad. They join voluntary organizations and specialized clubs – voluntarily not compulsorily. They are DIY exponents. They attend all manner of classes – literary, painting, health and keep fit, sometimes for fun, sometimes for formal study. They play games of all kinds. They read, look at the television screen, listen to the radio, go to plays, films and concerts.

Compare that with the circumstances of the vast majority of the population in the nineteenth century and consider the almost limitless range of opportunities people now have for learning informally. It is as obvious as it is startling. And the point about experiential learning is that most people take for granted whatever they may have learned through their activities. It is all locked up inside them. There is no external evidence that they have it. And because there is no external evidence, mostly they assume they have not got it.

For many people that does not matter. For an increasing number it does matter, although many of them do not know that it matters. It matters because through their discouraging experience of schooling they have come to think of themselves as non-learners. In many cases that means they undervalue themselves: a personal tragedy. As working individuals it matters because their effectiveness, their future as employees, depends increasingly on continuing to learn. Thinking you are not much good at learning is little encouragement for trying to learn more. It therefore matters for society. Since it is true that we now have an under-educated, relatively untrained workforce and that our economic wellbeing in the ever more competitive international system depends upon having a highly skilled workforce, the capacity for individuals to learn and their willingness to learn at any stage of life has become a critical question for preserving, let alone improving, our current standard of living. All that becomes of deeper significance at the individual level.

The only way known of tapping experiential learning is to think about it. Experience is all that people have when thinking about experiential learning. So the trick is to extract from experience what has been learned through reflecting systematically on that experience. There is a fourfold sequence for doing that, though the fourth stage is only necessary for those who are seeking formal recognition.

> Systematic reflection on experience for significant learning.
>
> Identification of significant learning, expressed in precise statements, constituting claims to the possession of knowledge and skills.
>
> Synthesis of evidence to support such claims.
>
> Assessment for accreditation.

Thinking about experience in this way involves, inevitably, thinking about self. If you think you are a poor learner, but come to realize that you have learned rather a lot, even though you did not think so, you are likely to think differently about yourself. So there is a very powerful self-assessment strand involved in this reflection. And that leads to something else. If you come to think of yourself differently because you have conducted a personal audit and were surprised at the result — you did not think you were that good —

like as not your confidence will soar. The way you present yourself will change. A sense of achievement, which now is there, may well transform the way you talk, act, think and even stand. And that can lead on to something quite different.

Motivation is a curious thing. What makes people do things? Whether it is because they want to or need to their action presupposes that they have some sense that they *can* do it. So whether you just want to or need to you are much more likely to try tackling something if you believe you have a good chance of succeeding. And that is precisely what experiential learning can give − the motivating sense of achievement.

At this point it is important to say that many individuals need some help over systematic reflection on experience. This key to the door of experiential learning sometimes needs searching out. In other words, to work through that fourfold sequence is not as straightforward as it may seem. Put differently, self-assessment is not something most people can just sit down and do. Someone else needs to be involved. That does not necessarily mean a physical presence. DIY handbooks are now available for identifying experiential learning, just as they are for building your own garage. Many universities and colleges have devised them for their students. The Learning from Experience Trust published *A Learner's Introduction to Building on Your Own Experience*. For nurses the *Open Learning* programme published with Macmillan can help. But the likelihood is that getting to the assessment stage will lead to all sorts of evaluation, so that help and support can extend to planning for the future. That may cover career planning, education planning, indeed life planning, for which some form of education and career counselling can be helpful.

Not everyone who sets out on the experiential learning track needs it. Some people can be so stimulated by the realization that they know more than they thought they knew that they have an immediate sense that some half-acknowledged dream can become true. With a clear destination they can move directly towards it. But for many there can be a sense of the world suddenly opening, presenting a whole range of unexpected choices which can feel confusing. The acknowledged half-dreamt dream can turn out to be the wrong one, even a nightmare, as the self-assessment alters the focus on the future. In that case support and help is not only desirable but well nigh essential. Friends and relatives can provide that support as well as anyone else in the initial stages, if the relationships are right. A group of men and women engaged in the same sequence of reflections can be best of all. Learning from one's peers is often the best way of learning. And this is just as true for eliciting learning from experience as it is for any other kind of learning.

Thus individual's reactions to self-assessment can range from the sudden realization that study of a particular kind is just the right thing, through a sense of career advancement which seems possible but previously was blocked by diffident uncertainty, to what is really a cry for help in making sense of a new world. The first individual may be so determined to pursue a goal which had never even seemed remotely possible, that prospectuses may be sent for, applications completed, money matters settled, all without any help. But help may be necessary to sort out what various prospectuses offer and to consider which college, university or adult centre might be the most congenial. And perhaps advisory interviews need to be arranged as a first step. Advisers or counsellors can provide the right kind of help where someone is interested primarily in qualifications.

If career advancement is the target, there can also be significant differences in the help that can be needed. This is a matter almost for a strengths and weaknesses audit, a kind of profit and loss accounting. In these cases systematic reflection on experience is likely to have revealed a number of accomplishments, stocks of knowledge and a range of skills beyond those required for the current job. This is the position of countless thousands of women in all categories of office roles. The sorting out of possibilities here involves comparing the talents, experience and capabilities of one individual with the requirements of a more responsible position. Maybe there is an opening in the present place of work, maybe it means looking elsewhere. Whatever the case, the point is that the way individuals present themselves for advancement may well become positive and replace a former attitude of ignoring possibilities out of lack of self-confidence. At this stage the role of an adviser can be crucial.

As for the third individual, who is confused, perhaps alarmed as well as excited by a sense of new opportunities, the task is to get a compass bearing on a future direction. This is a bit like drawing up the profit and loss account but without being able to make entries in the ledger of existing employment. And it needs time; time to come to terms with the contrast between the existing pattern of life and the abilities and interests shown by thinking about experience; time to order a new range of possibilities to a set of priorities; time to screw up courage to deal with all these things. Again the role of an adviser can be critical.

So whether experiential learning for individuals proves to be a route towards greater personal satisfaction or to qualifications or to employment or advancement, there is one common feature: one way and another it can represent a transition from some feeling of disappointment at a sense of under-achievement or failure to a sense of success and possibilities of greater fulfilment. In those terms, experiential learning is often a way of overturning or rather correcting the deficiencies of schools. By extension, therefore, the term experiential learning can be seen to offer a critique of the inadequacies of what formal state provision often presents to a large proportion of young people before they reach the age of sixteen.

However, experiential learning can be put to use for different purposes and at quite different levels. This is true for fully experienced people in employment. One of the major problems facing increasing numbers of people in employment in middle management and above is keeping abreast of the needs for quality performance. Just as it is now a fact of everyday experience that anyone may face a number of career changes during a working life, so something of the same is becoming prevalent within the same place of employment. Staff appraisal procedures are supposed to be a way of keeping job performance under regular review, but too often they are perfunctory exchanges, when items are checked off in little boxes and with relatively little discussion about performance. If experiential learning is introduced, then context and tone is transformed for official discussions about quality in employment and how to improve. This will be explored later (Chapter 8) but it is an important matter to log because of its significance for individuals.

APEL is much more than a sophisticated deficiency-level model of learning. It is positive. It is asserting pluses. It may imply drawing attention to minuses but that is incidental to the pluses. It delivers a message to all who can hear that there is a good chance that you are worth more than you think you are worth at present. Hence it is an issue of huge potential importance for society as a whole.

3

APEL and Higher Education

The attitude to APEL in higher education in the 1990s is very different from what it was when the topic was introduced in the early 1980s. Then it was seen as a rather dubious proposition; now, for many universities, it represents a highly significant institutional commitment.

Higher education was the first place where the assessment of experiential learning and its potential emerged in relation to formal education. As was to be expected, there was considerable scepticism. Many could not see how it would ever be a significant issue at all; others did not want to see that experiential learning had anything to do with them professionally. Indeed, for some the very idea was an affront.

Yet is is revealing to note that APEL can raise in a different context, and simultaneously, many of the issues which are endlessly debated in higher education: the criteria used to admit students, the characteristics of the student body and the work of admission tutors; the quality, content and presentation of prospectuses and publicity material; the arrangements for offering education and career advice to students; the content, organization and administration of academic programmes; pedagogy and the various ways of encouraging students to learn; assessment procedures and the nature of evidence required. Some of these topics lead inexorably to the relationship between part-time and full-time study, and so on to views about the various ways of being a student, and indeed to the ways in which institutions define their purpose.

The earliest discussions concerned APEL as an additional route for entry to higher education but this was not long the focus although APEL got assimilated to Access courses and occasionally was adopted to help recruit for courses that were finding it hard to attract sufficient numbers of students, such as engineering. From the beginning of the 1980s polytechnics and colleges associated with the Council for National Academic Awards were using CNAA's regulations to do more or less what universities had always done – admit whom they chose irrespective of any formal education requirements. But since most polytechnics and universities had long lists of applicants for almost every subject, there was no incentive for them to undertake the 'new-fangled' ideas of APEL. Rather those long application lists provided convenient screens from behind which to argue that APEL was too expensive a business to undertake, making heavy demands on staff already overloaded with teaching and administration.

So in the early 1980s experiential learning engaged the attention of higher education as a version of admission with advanced standing or exemption. Once people really began to think about it, it was obvious that there were bound to be men and women who had acquired knowledge and skill informally which might well be broadly similar to the content of sections of degree courses. If that proved to be the case, there was little point in requiring them to go through the motions of learning what they knew already. To make them do that – and there was ample evidence that it was happening – was wasteful of an institution's resources and students' time and money. Most serious of all, it was deeply demotivating for the students.

That case was proven (Evans, 1988) and some specific benefits came from the proving. It rapidly became obvious that awarding credit for experiential learning in degree programmes was more manageable when courses of study were organized in smaller sections. As it happened APEL arrived in the UK at the time when many institutions were beginning to debate the merits of adopting a modular, or unit-based, curriculum.

Assessment was the most critical academic issue. Whatever procedures were adopted, when it came to awarding academic credit towards a qualification, they had to be acceptable both to academic peers who served as internal examiners and to external examiners. Thus assessors of experiential learning had to feel absolutely secure that their results, and how they arrived at them, could withstand rigorous scrutiny from any and every quarter.

Wrestling with this challenge led to two other developments, one institutional, the other to do with curriculum structure and content. Clearly academic integrity was best assured when papers defining the rules and regulations under which APEL would be conducted were submitted to the relevant academic body in the institution and given formal approval. Submissions needed to cover the way students or applicants would be helped to formulate their claims for academic credit on the basis of experiential learning, as well as the methods of assessment. Also, which was very important, procedures needed to be established for handling any appeals which might be lodged by students with complaints to make (Storan, 1988).

The curriculum issues that APEL helped to bring into focus in the early 1980s were those of learning outcomes and learning agreements. The argument for introducing learning outcomes was that if the syllabus for a course of study included statements about what students were expected to know and be able to do at the end of the course, these would serve as a tool for assessors. But they would also serve as a ready reckoner for students submitting claims for experiential learning because these students would be able to refer to the learning outcomes of the area of study in which they thought they had already mastered the content. So both for students and academic staff learning outcomes were seen as a boon, not least as a way of saving time all round. And this debate ran through many institutions of higher education well before the National Council for Vocational Qualifications (NCVQ) produced its version of learning outcomes expressed as competences.

The issue of learning agreements related to the question of course content and its appropriateness or otherwise for older students. Since it was accepted that older students often arrived in higher education already equipped with some knowledge acceptable at degree level, what was to be the response if it emerged that what they wanted to continue to study did not feature in the way they wanted in the courses on offer? This would become a telling issue when teachers in higher education entered serious discussion with employers about forms of collaboration. But it was always a potentially telling factor for older students applying in the usual way.

Learning agreements came to be seen as a way of meeting this curriculum problem.

All of these issues connected with APEL added to the existing need for staff professional development. That is the topic of Chapter 10 but it is important to register that there was a change in role for many academic staff undertaking APEL activities: a shift from teaching to learning, to assessment and to counselling.

In March 1986 the issues under discussion were affected by the CNAA's launch of its Credit and Accumulation and Transfer Scheme (CATS). This was designed to enable men and women to bank the results of any study they undertook at either bachelor's or master's level in different institutions and at different times in their lives, subject to all the necessary rules to ensure the validity of their claims for academic credit and their appropriateness for the qualification they sought to obtain. To facilitate this scheme for credit accumulation CNAA established a CATS Registry in its headquarters as part of its national service.

APEL was a central feature of CATS from the beginning. Academic credit could be awarded for experiential learning for degree courses at both bachelor's and master's level. This had two immediate effects. The first was that it gave a national seal of approval to APEL. As the body responsible at that time for the academic approval and oversight of degree programmes being studied by over half the undergraduates in the United Kingdom, CNAA had used its full academic authority to declare that APEL was a valid and reliable feature in higher education.

The second result followed naturally. Very quickly some polytechnics followed CNAA's lead and began to develop their own schemes for credit accumulation and transfer, acting under the rubrics established by CNAA. This meant that there was a national service available for applicants who chose to go direct to the CNAA Registry with their experiential learning and also marked the beginnings of local services as more and more polytechnics worked out their own approaches to credit accumulation and transfer.

From the beginning it was part of the planning of credit accumulation and transfer that people in employment should be able to get academic credit for any courses which they attended, whether provided in-house by companies or attended elsewhere, possibly run by professional bodies, provided such courses met the necessary criteria.

The importance of this provision, which related directly to the increasing emphasis on collaboration with employers, was demonstrated very quickly in two ways after the establishment of the CNAA Registry and the emergence of institutions' own schemes. The first was in the validation and credit rating of companies' in-house courses for academic credit (Dearden, 1991b) and the second was in learning agreements for employees (Dearden, 1989). Both came in as direct results of the new arrangements created by credit accumulation and transfer for working towards higher education qualifications. And both were possible because of the way experiential learning had been incorporated in the CATS regulations.

The validation and credit rating of companies' in-house courses involved companies submitting courses for scrutiny by academic experts in the relevant field with a view to determining whether they were acceptable as study programmes for higher education in terms of content, level and assessment procedures. If they were, then credit points could be awarded. Once that was done it followed that any employee who had satisfactorily completed a credit-rated course could claim that amount of academic credit towards an appropriate qualification.

The negotiations to complete such arrangements were not as straightforward as that brief description might suggest. For employers they posed several complicated issues, which will be discussed in Chapter 8. But for higher education there were also delicate issues involved, largely to do with assessment. Most employers did not have assessment procedures for their in-house courses which could produce the kinds of results suited to the academic purposes of higher education. The successful outcome of a credit-rating exercise depended, therefore, on higher education and employers together devising mutually acceptable procedures. This was an important staff development experience for many academics, and it had considerable significance for the curriculum as well, both generally and in particular with collaborative schemes with employers and companies.

Learning agreements for employees was the other rapid development following the establishment of CATS. Using the opportunities opened up by credit accumulation and experiential learning, a scheme was devised whereby employees could negotiate a learning programme which met three requirements: it had to be what an employee wanted to study; equally it had to be something which was acceptable to an academic as meeting degree criteria; but it also had to be a programme of study both rooted in and forming an extension to day-to-day work. That was one source of potential credit towards a degree. Very quickly, however, it emerged that there were two other sources of credit which could be incorporated in a learning agreement. There were any credit ratings which had been awarded to the companies' in-house courses. And there was prior experiential learning: what had been learned during work life and leisure (Dearden, 1991a).

Somewhat to the surprise of many of those involved in the early developments of both credit ratings and learning agreements, it became clear that significant elements in the material which could be included were at post-graduate level. So APEL had piloted an additional route towards masters' as well as bachelors' degrees. What was more, if these opportunities for progression towards qualifications were academically acceptable for those in employment, they had to be equally acceptable for older students who might approach an institution directly, bringing their experiential learning with them. The connection was made with the curriculum point made earlier on.

Both the credit rating of in-house courses and learning agreements caught on fast. By the end of the 1980s some 50 employing organizations and professions, covering most occupations, including production industry, the financial services, the retail trade and public service and some professions, had negotiated credit rating agreements with a rapidly increasing number of institutions. And things did not stop there. Some collaborators went on to negotiate degree programmes which were tailormade to meet a company's particular requirements. Thus for some of those institutions a combination of APEL, the credit rating of companies' in-house courses and learning agreements became vital tools in forging new relationships with the world of work. It turned out that APEL was a many-headed creature.

Much of the experiential learning which featured in these arrangements with employers was prior in the sense that it had taken place before an employee was officially enrolled in an academic institution. But it was current where it featured as part of a learning programme which had been approved academically. These developments coincided with debates about sandwich courses.

Sandwich courses, which involve periods of work or field experience as part of a course of study, had been one of the fastest expanding categories of degree course since the 1960s. Most vocationally orientated studies had developed sandwich courses, notably engineering and business studies. They were popular with students and with employers. But they were more expensive because they lasted four years instead of three. During the 1980s the nagging question was often asked, what is the educational justification for sandwich courses? What do students actually learn during their work experience component? Could what they learn be assessed as part of their degree studies? How could those results be incorporated in the results for classified honours degrees? How could what they learn support the customary justification for sandwich courses: that they are an effective means of relating theory to practice? And were there ways of organizing the opportunities for learning during work experience so that students learned more (Ashworth and Saxton, 1992)?

All this was no more than seeking to put the assessment of experiential learning at the heart of the work experience component of sandwich courses. But it raised another question as well. Suppose the learning from work experience could be assessed and integrated with classified honours degrees, could it be seen as a way of getting the benefits of sandwich courses in less than four years?

No answer had materialized to that question by the end of the 1980s, but a different answer came from a different way of conceiving work experience within degree programmes. It was proved that within three-year, non-vocational, non-sandwich courses, there were ways of organizing, administering and supervising work experience so that students followed negotiated learning programmes and could have what they learned assessed, so that those assessments contributed to their end-of-course results (Alston, 1993). Whatever the long-term influence of this development, it is yet another indication of the power of the assessment of experiential learning in so many educational contexts.

So far there is no satisfactory answer to a related issue in higher education which can involve experiential learning; the questions which arise about the concept of competences as learning outcomes. There is increasing agreement that the inclusion in course syllabuses of learning outcomes, or learning intentions as some prefer to call them, is a helpful development for both academic staff and students. But there is little or no agreement about the nature of 'competences' as appropriate for higher education. Part of the problem is that the competences as developed by NCVQ are essentially vocational and occupationally specific. That was the Council's brief and forms part of a national attempt to increase the skills level and enhance the employability of the entire workforce. But that view of learning outcomes can only fit rather uncomfortably, if at all, in degree programmes, which, however vocational some of them may be, are not conceived as purely vocational since they are part of the far wider purposes of higher education.

However, there is another way of thinking about competences as a curriculum device for increasing the employability of those graduating before entering employment. And this is where APEL could become another issue. It is possible to produce broadly written competences which relate to general occupational areas, such as office and public administration, community and voluntary organizations, the retail trade, without these being related to particular course content. This could provide a convincing answer to the criticism often levelled at higher education that its concern for knowledge too often seems confined to an ability to reproduce taught material or, at best, to show an aptitude to review it critically or develop it. It is said that vocational competence is about the ability to perform in the real world of work. General occupational competences which could be acquired through any one of a variety of taught courses would be essentially concerned with applied knowledge. All the usual requirements for mastering knowledge would be upheld so there would be no question of devaluing the currency of a degree through lowering standards.

If any such scheme was developed, APEL would feature prominently. If competences were not tied to particular courses, they could be acquired in a variety of ways. Those ways would include learning from experience. And that would mean that people in full-time or part-time work, as well as full-time or part-time students following taught courses, could well be meeting the necessary criteria for a particular competence. This will seem very close to the ideas of NCVQ. The difference lies in the understanding of the concept of competence.

Running through every one of these developments stemming from the assessment of experiential learning is the overriding question of quality. On the one hand, higher education institutions have to ensure and guard their academic integrity; their reputations depend on it, and nothing is more important than that at a time when they are all being exhorted to compete with one another for students. Academic audits for quality assurance are conducted by the Higher Education Quality Council to monitor this nationally. Furthermore, quality assessment is part of the brief from government to the Higher Education Funding Council. An in-stitution's funding can be at risk if its academic quality is considered inadequate. This is a highly contentious matter. Its importance for APEL is obvious.

But questions of quality affect every part of an institution's work – admissions, student support, course structure and content, teaching and learning methods, assessment and examination procedures, institutional management and internal resourcing, and – above all – leadership. Thus APEL is also relevant to the Division of Academic Audit of the Higher Education Quality Control. Quality is not merely an audit of degree results. It is a matter of everything an institution does and how it does it. Experiential learning connects with all those considerations (Robertson, 1994).

REFERENCES

Alston, Philomena et al. (1993): *Work-based Learning for Academic Credit: Non-vocational Three-year Degrees*. London: Learning from Experience Trust.

Ashworth, Peter and Saxton, Judy (1992): *Managing Work Experience*. London: Routledge.

Dearden, Gerald (1989): *Learning While Earning: Learning Contracts for Employees*. London: Learning from Experience Trust.

Dearden, Gerald (1991a): *The Assessment of Prior Learning: An Intro-duction for Employers, Employees and Academic Assessors*. London: Learning from Experience Trust.

Dearden, Gerald (1991b): *The Credit-Rating of In-company Courses: How to Get Double Value*. London: Learning from Experience Trust.

Evans, Norman (1984): *Access to Higher Education: Non-standard Entry to CNAA's First Degrees and DipHE Courses* London: CNAA.

Evans, Norman (1988): *The Assessment of Prior Experiential Learning*. London CNAA.

Robertson, David (1994): *Choosing to Change: Extending Access, Choice and Mobility in Higher Education*. London: HEQC.

Storan, John (1988): *Making Experience Count*. London: Learning from Experience Trust.

Turner, Anthony and Evans, Norman (1993): *The Potential of the Assessment of Experiential Learning in Universities*. London: Learning from Experience Trust.

4

APEL and Further Education

The assessment of prior and experiential learning is important for further education colleges because it can serve almost as a litmus test for their capacity to cope with the new role they have as incorporated institutions. Funded directly by a central government funding agency, the Further Education Funding Council (FEFC) and its regional committees, severed from the local education authorities which had responsibility for them until 1 April 1993, they have to learn to be thoroughly independent, to stand alone without local support of the kind they have been accustomed to. What is more they have to find ways of achieving student targets to justify levels of funding from the FEFC that will sustain them as viable institutions. And, beyond that, they have to find ways of attracting additional income since they have been told that FEFC funds will be controlled tightly so that there is no financial slack in the system. All in all, any further education college now knows that to survive it has to learn to live on the high wire of competition. APEL, which encompasses not only different ways of learning but of being students, has become a vital matter for further education.

The first time staff in further education took any notice of the significance of experiential learning for assessment was in 1980, when Jack Mansell, then Chief Officer of the Further Education Unit, reviewed *The Knowledge Revolution*, a book that introduced the ideas of experiential learning to Britain (Evans, 1980). That resulted in *Curriculum Opportunity*, a survey of entry qualifications for courses offered by further education to see how far they accepted or excluded experiential learning (Evans, 1982). That publication, which was distributed to every further and higher education institution in the country, served notice that experiential learning was something to take note of for the future.

The second move of significance was when Alun Davies, then (1982) Chief Inspector for higher and further education in the Inner London Education Authority, recognized that some of the curriculum and staff development implications of experiential learning could help further education colleges change their ways, which, longsightedly, he saw they were going to have to do in the future. And having spotted its significance he briefed some of his seconded staff in the Curriculum Development Unit of ILEA to do what they could to promote the theory and practice of experiential learning in ILEA's further education colleges.

Some colleges took up experiential learning enthusiastically, particularly with reference to access courses, which were designed to provide a route for older students into higher education. Quickly tutors discovered the truth of the claim that students gain in confidence when they discover their unsuspected learning achievements. And on the tail of this usual approach to access courses came a specific development in connection with admission to a social science course. Tutors were asked to write down what knowledge, skills and capacities they were actually looking for when they considered applications. The access course was then organized around those requirements, and provided opportunities for students to use their experiential learning assessments to meet them. In some ways that was a precursor to NCVQ.

And that is how things stood in further education until the National Council for Vocational Qualifications (NVCQ) was established in 1986. In various parts of the country APEL activities developed as individual enthusiasts heard about it through the various networks that staff belong to, and as some of the ILEA staff moved out to other parts of the country. The Further Education Unit maintained its interest through publishing two further volumes on APEL: *The Assessment of Experiential Learning* and *Case Studies on the Assessment of Experiential Learning* (Evans, 1987a and b). The Learning from Experience Trust issued two publications for staff development (Gorringe, 1987; Gorringe et al., 1987). But as with other sections of the education service,

APEL remained something which either did or did not commend itself for attention.

What transformed the attitude in further education was the arrival of the NCVQ. Not straight away, because that is not the way things happen in education, but a fuse was ignited which could not readily be doused. NCVQ is neither a curriculum unit nor is it an examining body; it is a verifying body for certifying that qualifications offered by other bodies merit the award of national vocational qualifications based on occupational competences as defined by Industry Lead Bodies and authorized for use by NCVQ itself.

Now the essential characteristic of NCVQ's competences is that they are separated utterly from courses of study. NCVQ's concern begins and ends with the question, does this candidate have or not have this particular competence? The connection with prior learning assessment is immediately obvious. In theory anyone can offer themselves for assessment for a particular competence or a unit of a competence at any time without attending any course anywhere. And that is just another way of talking about APEL being applied at will. Or rather the assessment of prior achievement, APA, as NCVQ chose to call it.

Unfortunately for the smooth running of further education colleges, the awarding bodies are involved in these arrangements for assessing NVQs, and particularly when using APEL. Each of them – the main ones being the Business and Technology Council (BTEC), City and Guilds and the Royal Society of Arts (RSA) – all have their own regulations which need to be followed when using assessments of experiential learning towards one of their qualifications. And since it is those qualifications which have been kite-marked by NCVQ for certain competences, this is a matter of high significance.

Complaints abound. Regulations get changed without adequate notice, landing colleges in difficulties. Although the approval is there for assessing experiential learning, the procedures are too bureaucratic and protracted and, incidentally, too expensive. Inconsistencies exist, it is claimed, between moderators from the same examining body. Further, it is sometimes suggested that some moderators are relatively ignorant about the theory and practice of experiential learning and its assessment so they hide behind regulations and apply their own interpretations of them, rather than abiding by the spirit in which they were promulgated by the awarding body. In these ways, then, APEL can be a trying issue for some staff in further education colleges.

If that was all there was to it, further education colleges would be free to go their own way as before, ignoring APEL for accreditation if they chose to, though they are unlikely to be able to ignore it for admissions. But there is a great deal more to it. And that great deal more relates directly to the funding issues which confront them for the future.

No doubt the formulae will be changed as the new system gets established, but it is clear that there will be connections between levels of funding and numbers of NVQs achieved by students. Gone are the days when enrolments at the beginning of an academic year established institutional budget entitlements, however many of those enrolled students completed or did not complete their courses. And because of another provision in the reforms for funding further education, financial support for the many forms of adult education which, historically, further education has provided is either withdrawn absolutely, or reduced, or subject to increasingly uncertain decisions about discretionary awards and general funding.

Nor is this the end of the way in which NVQs could well affect the funding of further education in the future. Beginning with schemes of Training Credits for Youth Employment programmes and extending to Training Credits for Adult Employment Schemes, NVQs are being used as criteria for assessing budget entitlements not only for those further education colleges which continue to offer such programmes but for the Training and Enterprise Councils which now have the responsibility for administering and funding those managers they commission to run the programmes. This means that colleges are to be paid in part at least for running those programmes according to the number of NVQs the participants achieve. Failure to meet the target number of passes will mean that they do not get paid the full amount of their contract. Similarly, TECs are liable to have their budgets reduced by the Department of Employment if in turn they do not deliver the number of NVQs they predicted would be achieved in their own area. In other words, NVQs have become a mechanism for a sophisticated system of payment by results, borrowed and adapted from the nineteenth century. For further education this presents the difficult choice between agreeing to contracts on those terms because they need the income, or not even attempting to secure contracts because they might actually lose money instead of earning it. APEL is an important factor in making that decision.

So NVQs are being used as a financial engine for driving a large part of the further education system. A large part only, because it cannot be said too often that the work of further education colleges is not, never has been and should never be contained by definitions of what constitute for employers and NCVQ acceptable occupational competences. But that large part of their work which is concerned with vocational education and training leading to NVQs is now subject to the financial provisions outlined, and so APEL becomes a very important consideration for colleges as they try to work out where their income is going to come from.

Quite how all that is going to be affected by the introduction of General National Vocational Qualifications (GNVQs) is by no means clear. If the drive is successful to establish GNVQs as a parallel qualification to A-levels, and of equal status, colleges are going to be offering both qualifications. If it turns out that the assessment of prior and experiential learning features in the arrangements for GNVQs, then further complications are bound to arise.

A new development which is following from the 1990 Education Reform Act is more extensive collaboration between further education colleges and higher education. Franchising arrangements are being established in most parts of the country whereby parts of diploma and first degree courses are taught in further education colleges under the academic authority of a university or college of higher education. Given the relatively rapid introduction of APL and APEL provision in higher education, franchising necessarily means that some further education colleges will need to devise comparable schemes of their own.

For further education colleges these developments pose some exceedingly difficult institutional issues, and this is where APEL begins to become a controversial business. Just how problematic and controversial becomes obvious when the organization, administration and management of a college is seen from the principal's desk as he/she goes over budgets with the financial controller as they prepare for the next governors' meeting. At the back of their minds all the time is the fact that their governing body is now financially responsible — if the college goes bankrupt, it is the governors who will be responsible.

For the college as a whole it means that all the budget lines for the costs of academic, administrative and support staff, running costs — including staff development, library, laboratories, student services as well as annual maintenance of buildings and equipment and capital expenditure — have to be balanced against finely calculated sources of income (Field, 1993).

This is where APEL becomes such a critical factor, because it introduces many more ways of enrolling students than simply signing them up for regular courses. It introduces additional ways of recruiting students from sections of the population which are under-represented and often under-served at present; minority groups of all kinds (Peters and McKelvey, 1993). Each and every student appearing in the college's records system represents income. APEL means that the former sharp distinction between full-time and part-time students can be removed. At its simplest, on the basis of experiential learning students can be credited for parts of courses. Assessing experiential learning for NCVQ competences is less simple. Where a candidate meets the requirements for some units of a competence but not all of them, the college needs to be able to provide 'top up' opportunities so that the candidate can learn to meet the requirements of the missing units.

More complex still is where a college looks for collaboration schemes with employers. Some employers are wanting to use NVQs as part of their own training efforts. Some want to use the qualifications offered under the Management Charter Initiative. Some are not at all concerned with those kinds of qualifications but are most concerned to find ways of developing the effectiveness of their workforce. Many want to establish their employee training programmes so that they meet the requirements of Investors in People. Whatever the employer's chosen way of attempting to maintain, if not increase, the company's profitability through training and skill enhancement, a college negotiating for a contract can present APEL as an attractive option.

Work-based learning is one way of making APEL an attractive idea for an employer. What employees have learned from and through their work can be assessed, and whether those assessments are used for formal qualifications or not, their experiential learning is the foundation for acquiring whatever knowledge and skill the employer needs them to have for the future. Thus an employer is getting a double benefit from the work he pays people to do. They earn their keep with him. They also learn things which can be exploited for re-training and skill enhancement.

It may well be though, and this tends to apply to larger rather than smaller and medium-sized businesses, that the employer has a range of in-house training programmes for employees. These too can come into the experiential learning bracket. By arrangement between employer and college, in-house courses can be evaluated for possible credit towards public qualifications without any reference to NCVQ. Again, seen from the employer's viewpoint that looks like getting double value for money. The courses the company needed for its own purposes become part of an award-bearing course as approved academically for that purpose.

In some cases all of those possibilities can be worked up into a series of learning agreements, which give employer, employee and college firm control over the agreed content of the training course. This can be a vital way of ensuring the quality of the arrangements made. And, for the college, it will provide the kind of evidence that will count with the FEFC when it comes to deciding on college budget allocations.

These are just some of the variations which can be played on the experiential learning theme. It is alway a theme with two motifs: extending service to potential learners, and money. Whatever the professional sensibilities about public education moving in this direction, it is the direction which government policies have enshrined in statute, and colleges have no option but to comply. APEL offers a particular route towards compliance while keeping the marketplace mentality firmly in its place.

Those professional sensibilities lead into considering some of the controversial aspects to APEL. For it is one thing to show how colleges can make the best use of it in their new way of working; it is quite another to turn ideas into day-to-day operation (Challis, 1993).

Admission procedures have to be changed: a college has to be ready to register students who have no interest in pursuing a full-time course, or regular part-time courses either, but come for limited purposes of their own requiring relatively small amounts of formal tuition but considerably more time on being advised and helped. Staff time will also be required for assessing for experiential learning.

It follows from that that a college which intends to take APEL seriously needs to reorganize its student services arrangements to take full account of the new demands this wider clientele of students will make on it. And if the prime objective is to attract as many potential students to the college as possible, then it is essential to provide some form of reception area where men and women can feel welcome and safe to ask questions without commitment. Given the need to attract additional categories of students, anything which will put them off, starting from their first contact with the college (especially by phone), is an expensive mistake.

The impact of all of this on administrative and support staff is clear. They play a vital part in altering the public stance of the college. It means treating members of the public who come to the college more as 'customers and clients' who are considering whether college can offer them what they want, rather than people who come to inquire about the regulations for enrolling on courses published in a prospectus. The change cannot come about by fiat; a carefully evolved staff development programme is necessary.

The impact is just as great for academic staff. While many will continue to teach what they have been accustomed to teach, they are likely to find that their courses are reordered into modules or units as a means of accommodating a wider variety of needs. Not all academic staff relish that kind of change. But some of them will find that less of their time is spent on teaching, and more is spent on being general facilitators of students' learning through advising, supporting and evaluating their work. As a result, the role of departments may well change. And again that is not to everyone's liking. So just as for administrative and support staff a programme of staff development is essential (Henebery, 1992).

There are two other factors in further education at work which relate to APEL: credit-based curricula and franchising. Urgent discussions, sponsored by the FEU and the Higher Education Quality Council, are in train about the possibility of establishing some kind of nationally agreed credit-based system. It is seen as a means of establishing progression routes within and between institutions; as a way of facilitating curriculum planning within a college; as a means of measuring added value in education; as a mechanism for improving accountability and as a means of analysing stages and levels within courses (FEU, 1992, 1993; Robertson, 1994). APEL is integral to each and every one of those considerations.

The franchising of parts of degree courses by universities to colleges again has to involve APEL. If a degree course offered by the responsible university includes provision for APEL, then it follows that the college-teaching part of that course will also have to provide facilities for APEL. How significant this aspect of franchising becomes for further education depends on the stop/go/stop pronouncements by the Department for Education about numbers in higher education.

Thus every part of a further education college's activity, perhaps even its very life, is likely to be affected if and when APEL is assimilated to its mainstream work.

REFERENCES

Challis, Maggie (1993): *Introducing APL*. London: Routledge.

Evans,Norman(1980):*TheKnowledgeRevolution*.London:GrantMcIntyre.

Evans, Norman (1983): *Curriculum Opportunity: A Map of Experiential Learning in Entry Requirements for Further and Higher Education Award-bearing Courses*. London: FEU.

Evans, Norman (1987a): *The Assessment of Experiential Learning*. London: FEU.

Evans, Norman (1987b): *Case Studies in the Assessment of Experiential Learning*. London: FEU.

Field, Michael (1993): *APL: Developing Flexible Colleges*. London: Routledge.

FEU (1992, 1993): *A Basis for Credit?* London: Further Education Unit.

Gorringe, Richard (1987): *Handbook for the Assessment of Experiential Learning*. London: Learning from Experience Trust/Avon Education Dept.

Gorringe, Richard, Henebery, Corinne, et al. (1987): *Resource Materials for the Assessment of Experiential Learning*. London: Learning from Experience Trust/Avon Education Dept.

Henebery, Corinne (1992): *Assessment of Prior Learning and Learner Services*. London: FEU.

Peters, Helen and McKelvey, Cecilia (1993): *APL for the Whole Community*. London: Routledge.

Robertson, David (1994): *Choosing to Change: Extending Access, Choice and Mobility in Higher Education*. London: HEQC.

5

APEL and Adult Education

Adult educators have always used the experiential learning of adult students. It is a basic tenet of their methodology. All their students are volunteers, becoming students simply because they wish to. If they are not satisfied with what they get, they depart. So the experience they bring with them is always a vital ingredient of the curriculum. It not only enlivens the study itself; it is an important motivating factor. Any account of the development of adult education makes this clear, whether it is the nineteenth-century story of working men's clubs, Tawney's inspiration for university extramural work, the Workers' Educational Association or the more recent and remarkable developments through Adult Education Institutes; the significance of the students' personal experience is a consistent thread.

But the assessment of experiential learning in any formal sense was not until very recently part of the story. For adult education it is and always has been a point of prime principle that learning is for its own sake and has no direct connection with award-bearing courses leading to qualifications. So when APEL came onto the agenda at the beginning of the 1980s, the attitude of the few adult educators who took part in discussions ranged from cautious to outright hostile.

The issue assessment posed for them was fundamental, and it remains so. It was this. The invitation to an adult to reflect on experience with a view to identifying what has been learned for some formal assessment is one thing; it is quite another for an individual to run the risk of being told that their learning is not acceptable for that formal purpose. That would represent rejection of a particularly personal kind since it would be based on a significant part of their life. Putting personal experience on the line could end by making it seem that an individual's very life was being rejected – and this despite tutors' intention to increase students' sense of self-value.

This was a sharply focused view of an issue which runs throughout considerations of experiential learning, whatever its context. But for adult education it first became a serious issue during the planning and then running of 'Making Experience Count'. The staff members from the Continuing Education unit at Thames Polytechnic (now the University of Greenwich) and the Department of Continuing and Community Education at Goldsmiths' College who launched MEC had to come to terms with it from the beginning (Storan, 1988).

There was also an institutional reason for experiential learning being seen in a different way by adult education. The 1980s was just as turbulent a period for adult education as it was higher and further education. In 1982 the last report of the Advisory Committee on Adult and Continuing Education (ACACE), chaired by Richard Hoggart, recommended that the Secretary of State should establish a central development agency to promote wider participation by adults in education (ACACE, 1982). Mark Carlisle, now Lord Carlisle, then the Secretary of State for Education and Science, rejected that idea, saying it was too costly a proposal. Instead, during the next two years there emerged three separate government-funded initiatives, each with a brief to serve adults in a different way.

There was the Professional and Industrial and Commercial Improvement Programme (PICKUP), which was designed to encourage higher and further education institutions to work out collaborative schemes with employers to develop the skills and knowledge of employees. There was the Return to Employment Programme (REPLAN), which was an initiative to help the unemployed get back to work. And the Unit for the Development of Adult and Continuing Education (UDACE). This last was to examine areas of possible development in the education of adults, recommend strategies for development and sponsor projects to encourage developments. Given the mounting expenditure by those three bodies over the years it could seem that it was government control rather than money which was the prime consideration in rejecting the ACACE line of thinking. Together those three bodies had a wide-ranging influence on services for adults for a decade, but by 1992 all of them had been abandoned as separate activities. REPLAN was scrapped by government decision and its work for the unemployed assimilated with other government-funded initiatives for adult training, run through the Department of Employment. UDACE was drafted into the Further Education Unit. PICKUP was assimilated by the two Funding Councils.

The effect of these developments on those who had thought of themselves as the main providers of adult education was extensive. REPLAN had money for funding schemes to tackle adult unemployment and was open to relevant proposals from any institution or group. This meant that local education authorities, either directly or in concert with their further education colleges, could apply, as could colleges directly, where local education authorities permitted this. So could independent training organizations and consultancies. So while some adult educators found themselves working on REPLAN projects it was not work which formed a coherent part of an adult service in the way that ACACE had recommended. For adult education it represented something of a threat.

PICKUP was different. This was a programme designed to stimulate further and higher education to contribute more energetically and imaginatively to helping industry and commerce become more competitive. And it worked, if the number of funded projects and the amount of money spent on them is anything to go by. Universities, polytechnics and colleges developed PICKUP units to handle this new category of work. It became big business for many of them. True, it was pump-priming funding, short-term contract work, but it was money, and during the 1980s any source of additional funding became increasingly important. So, as with REPLAN, this was an initiative which worked, but for those in the participating institutions who had worked in adult education as a career, it was something of a problematic development. Having more to do with continuing professional development than with traditional adult education, PICKUP could be seen as the start of assimilating adult into continuing education – a development which could have profound institutional implications.

Neither REPLAN nor PICKUP were significant for developments in the assessment of experiential learning. Some REPLAN projects used some of the principles that were being worked out in further education, particularly those managed through the FEU. The PICKUP programme at first took little interest, though at the turn of the decade it was beginning to do so.

Taken together, these two initiatives added to the general disturbance being felt by adult education as local education authorities struggled with their own funding problems resulting from government pressure to reduce expenditure. As a discretionary activity, adult education became increasingly at risk, not only for the funding of its staff and premises but for the discretionary grants available for individuals who might want to participate. The general effect was to increase uncertainty over the nature of the services for adults that would attract secure funding. There was also the question of whether any of those services would continue to be offered through adults education institutes, or whether what had been a separate service would become part of further education. This was hardly a promising seed bed for experiential learning and its assessment.

In 1984 UDACE entered this arena. And straightaway there was a distinct change of tone and concern about the involvement of adult education in the assessment of prior experiential learning. Access was one of UDACE's earliest preoccupations and inevitably APEL was part of that preoccupation. Based in the National Institute of Adult and Continuing Education, UDACE spawned a number of committees where members came from all parts of the country, from both statutory and voluntary organizations, and from the National Association of Teachers in Higher and Further Education (NATFHE) and the Further Education Unit. Thus not only did interest spread, so did active engagement.

For UDACE access became an all-embracing notion and led to systematic investigation of the entire range of factors which presented barriers to adults who wished to participate in study at any and every level (UDACE, 1990). So APEL featured in questions of advice and guidance (UDACE, 1986a), of finance (UDACE, 1986b), as well as institutional responses to adults who did not necessarily possess standard education qualifications or who were probably reluctant to approach formal education, if not downright hostile to the very idea. This was a major concern when investigating the factors which appeared to dissuade members of ethnic minorities and women from using the available opportunities. So APEL became a significant factor in developments intended to dismantle the barriers to wider participation in adult education.

One of the most important of those developments was the arrival of Open College federations and networks. These were a device for trying to engage adults who would not go anywhere near formal education institutions on their own initiative but whose keenness to study could be tapped, if they were engaged on their own terms. One of the ways of doing that was to use the principles and practice of APEL. Accrediting experiential learning provided a powerful motivation for the adults the Open College federations were trying to serve. It was also a tool for articulating the relations between Open College federations and further and higher education. It was a particular way of approaching Access (FEU, 1993).

Once the National Council for Vocational Qualifications began to publish its vocational competences and to adopt its own interpretations of APEL, and the examining and awarding bodies produced their own rules for handling the assessment of experiential learning, adult education was bound to be affected. This was particularly so for the Open College federations and all the varieties of outreach work which had resulted in part from REPLAN. Having worked out ways of accrediting experiential learning with further and higher education, either singly or in some form of consortium, the arrival of occupational competences in further education meant trying to achieve some accommodation between the achievements of Open College students and NCVQ's national vocational competences. And that could not be easy. Whereas NCVQ was concerned only with occupational competences, giving recognition for particular work roles, OCNs went beyond that, recognizing and acknowledging that for adult learners the vocational v. non-vocational distinction could be artificial achievements not necessarily related to a specific work role. So as well as trying to forge effective collaborative arrangements with the examining and awarding bodies, OCNs had to co-operate with NCVQ in the interests of their students. A National Open College Network was formed. Through it Open Colleges managed to collaborate directly with the Department for Education, NCVQ, the FEU and OU and the two funding Councils. And at the heart of all such negotiations, there was the assessment of prior and experiential learning. The funding implications referred to in Chapter 4 made this a critical matter. So far no satisfactory resolution has been found.

Nowhere was this more clear than for unpaid work. No-one disputes that unpaid work can be a rich source of learning. No-one doubts that one of the ways of increasing adult participation in formal learning is to enable people who have learned from their unpaid work to have formal recognition for it, if that is what they want. Before the appearance of NCVQ, efforts were being made to see how the kinds of learning which are likely to be acquired through unpaid work could become creditworthy in further and higher education. But given the way that NVQs will alter so much of what further education does and how it is funded, then as for the work of Open Colleges, some way has to be found of relating learning from unpaid work with occupational competences as approved by NCVQ. By definition, much of the learning from unpaid work is experiential. Its assessment therefore becomes a vital issue (Butler, 1991). This is especially so for voluntary bodies like the Women's Institute and the Citizens' Advice Bureau.

Experiential learning is a feature of adult life. Whenever adults set out to learn more about anything, what they have learned from previous experience is potentially important. The task of those who work professionally to promote adult learning is to determine how to harness the lessons of past experience for the benefit of all concerned. To that extent the assessment of experiential learning is in principle no different for adult education than for any other part of the post-secondary school provision. It is the context which is different.

REFERENCES

ACACE (1982): *Continuing Education: From Policies to Practice*. Leicester: Advisory Committee for Adult and Continuing Education.

Butler, Linda (1991): *Unpaid Work: The Developing Potential for Accreditation*. London: Learning from Experience Trust.

FEU (1993): *Open College Networks: Participation and Progression*. London: Further Education Unit.

Storan, John (1988): *Making Experience Count*. London: Learning from Education Trust.

UDACE (1986a): *The Challenge for Change: Educational Guidance for Adults*. Leicester: Unit for the Development of Adult and Continuing Education.

UDACE (1986b): *Financial Barriers to Access*. Leicester: Unit for the Development of Adult and Continuing Education.

UDACE (1990): *An Agenda for Access*. Leicester: Unit for the Development of Adult and Continuing Education.

6

APEL and the Professions

Experiential learning concerns the professions at different levels: qualifying courses, post-qualifying or post-experience courses membership and licence to practise. Since the 1980s the context for those concerns has changed radically. And this is largely because of the demise of the CNAA.

As greater and greater emphasis was put on continuing professional development during the 1980s, so experiential learning could not be ignored. Anyone interested in why employers were often unenthusiastic about higher education's contribution to the development of their professional employees encountered the frequent accusation that the institutions failed to provide what employers actually wanted. Some of the course content offered was either merely a repetition of what employees already knew or it was irrelevant. Any post-experience course will be successful to the extent that it begins where the participants actually are, not where some course designer considers they are or ought to be.

That maxim implies that the assessment of participants' experiential learning ought to be the foundation of any professional development provision. That may seem too idealistic, too demanding a way of organizing post-experience courses. However, an entirely realistic application of the assessment of experiential learning is an essential condition for success: awarding academic recognition and credit towards a further professional qualification on the basis of what has been learned already. Not doing this is not only an unprofessional waste of time and money, it is insulting to the professional as a student.

Once the CATS Registry was established by CNAA with full provision for experiential learning to be creditable at both bachelor's and master's degree levels, there was no difficulty in principle for higher education institutions to proceed along those lines for both qualifying and post-qualifying courses. And some did. That meant that the issue of experiential learning was dealt with at first degree and qualifying level.

The difficulty was, and is, that some professional bodies did not recognize experiential learning for their own awarding systems and so were reluctant to recognize the professional validity of courses provided by other bodies which incorporated experiential learning assessments. For those promoting APEL, this was like easing the way past one gate-keeper, only to find another barring the way. Broadly speaking that is where things stood with most professional bodies in the mid-1980s.

The employers' interest in credit accumulation for their employees generally began to change attitudes. And as with so many instances with APEL, at first the impulse to accept it came indirectly. During the validation and credit rating of some companies' in-house courses, it turned out that some were using courses offered by professional bodies for their own internal purposes. So when some of those courses offered by professional bodies were assigned academic credit under the APEL banner, technically experiential learning had been incorporated in some professional courses. And when higher education institutions accepted those ratings for credit towards degrees, including master's degrees, and when they were using assessments of prior experiential learning for credit as well, there began what in retrospect could look like a movement to outflank some professional bodies. But looks can belie reality. That fact that courses offered by a professional body had been credit rated in relation to a higher education award did not necessarily mean that the award could command professional recognition from that same professional body.

The issue about experiential learning in relation to professional recognition is the age-old one; tension between academic institutions and professional bodies over the content of courses carrying with them that professional recognition. Generally speaking, it is fair comment that in curriculum development many professional bodies had lagged behind academic institutions. And since experiential learning can pose problems for some academics, it is hardly

surprising that some officials and members of professional institutes found acceptance of experiential learning hard, given their
entirely proper and responsible concern for professional standards.
Fundamentally, this is a dispute about the quality of higher education qualifications. And the oddity of it is that some of the
academic staff who teach the degree courses are the same people
who sit on the professional bodies' committees which query the
quality of those courses.

Early on in the 1980s something of these difficulties had become
evident when the Youth Service tried to find ways of recognizing
for credit some of the on-the-job learning of unqualified youth
workers who were seeking a professional qualification. From the
mid-1980s onwards professionals in the health service and social
work began moves which lead to the incorporation of experiential
learning in their mainstream provision. The Institute of Building
Construction and the Employers Engineering Federation began
explorations, as did some professional institutes associated with
the financial services. Thus the climate of opinion about experiential learning and its assessment was changing in professional
bodies.

But the critical stage in the development for APEL with the professional bodies came through CNAA's CATS Registry. Beginning
in 1986 a number of professions (the Forensic Society, the Institute
of Supervisory Management, the Institute of Personnel Management, the Chartered Association of Certified Accountants and
some others) sought formal academic recognition for the courses
that they offered. Other bodies, such as the Brewers' Society, and
the Institute of Bankers and the Institute of Health Service Management, followed suit and obtained academic recognition from
polytechnics (as they then were). This did not necessarily mean,
as mentioned already, that they would all accept for professional
membership candidates who had completed degrees incorporating
APEL. But it was a significant move.

Towards the end of the 1980s the United Kingdom Central
Council for the Education and Training of Midwives and Nurses
(UKCC) launched exhaustive consultations about and preparation
of schemes for post-qualifying courses which emerged as their
Post Registration Education Programmes (PREP). This led to a
realization that a credit accumulation system was a necessary way
of trying to provide a cost-effective system. But the report also

resulted in the assessments of experiential learning being fully integrated in the new PREP proposals. Once the recommendations of that report were accepted, providers of PREP programmes up and down the country began to equip themselves for handling experiential learning. That concerned only post-initial qualifications. The story of initial qualifications was different.

Despite serious and protracted deliberations over the desirability of introducing assessments of prior experiential learning for entry to initial courses leading to registration, and despite being urged by the Secretary of State to do so, the UKCC took no action. Time alone will show whether that was a wise or a foolishly short-sighted decision. The English National Board, however, introduced provision for APEL in conversion courses which enable state enrolled nurses to become RGNs as the qualification for admission to the General Register for Nurses. It also urged nursing colleges to organize their courses on a modular basis within a credit accumulation system and to develop APEL procedures for their post-qualifying provision.

At the same time the National Health Training Authority (now the NHS Training Directorate) was developing a whole range of courses, largely funded by PICKUP, covering the training needs of all NHS employees: maintenance, financial, support and management, nursing and medical staff. Exactly the same issue arose: how to get proper recognition for what people had learned through their work and for themselves. APEL by any other name. For an organization which is the largest employer in Europe, this was an issue of huge financial importance. A good deal of its effort went into trying to obtain academic credit for a range of development courses which it had produced for itself and to obtain professional recognition for them. And of course experiential learning was part of that provision.

Another major actor in the professional field for experiential learning was the Central Council for Education and Training in Social Work (CCETSW). It was the possibilities offered by credit accumulation and transfer which attracted attention, and as with nursing, almost inexorably the assessment of prior experiential learning became a consideration. By 1992 there had been two important developments. When the regulations were published for the new Diploma of Social Work (DipSW) to replace the Certificate of Qualification in Social Work (CQSW) they included provision for assessments of experiential learning to be credited towards that new qualification.

There is a significant twist to these arrangements. CCETSW negotiated with CNAA for the two-year DipSW, as a two-year course, to be equivalent to a Diploma of Higher Education and carry two years' academic credit towards a bachelor's degree. So the professional decision taken by CCETSW about the validity of experiential learning for its own course, the DipSW, was buttressed by academic recognition at a national level from CNAA. This meant that a professional body charged with responsibility for ensuring standards in a very large professional service through the approval and oversight of courses leading to professional recognition had enshrined APEL in its regulations for initial training, which in this case carries with it a licence to practise.

The inclusion of experiential learning in the DipSW was one of CCETSW's moves. The other was with post-qualification provision. As with nursing and, indeed, with an increasing number of occupational bodies, the economics of keeping professional staff up-to-date presents a huge problem. Government is always urging the need to ensure improvements in professional standards, sometimes out of panic at some public scandal. It does very little to provide the resources for doing so. Attention therefore focuses on ways and means of providing and financing post-experience development courses. Seconding staff for full-time courses brings the double expense of paying for a staff replacement as well as the salary and course costs for the person seconded. So credit accumulation becomes a vital element and it brings with it the need to include the assessment of experiential learning.

However, for social work, especially at post-qualifying level, the assessment of experiential learning requires sophisticated approaches to delicate questions of professional practice. There is the question of acceptable evidence for assessment. Professional ethics enter when some of the evidence required may be available only through observation of interviews, some of which may prove to be confidential. There is the potentially contentious issue of determining who can properly conduct assessments. There are potentially explosive relationships between agency employers and academic institutions.

One approach to solving some of these issues is to develop a number of competences which combine both professional and academic requirements. Where they are written in terms which practitioners, employers and academic staff can accept, then competences can serve as a usable tool for assessing experiential learning. Achieving that requires an exceptionally high level of collaboration between Social Services Agency and academic institution. APEL plays a pivotal role in achieving that collaboration. For the employer it is almost as if, at last, justice is being done to the practitioner. For some academics the level of professional expertise that practitioners have developed comes as a revelation.

However, this is only the beginning of the story. It is too early to say what will be the long-term impact on other professional bodies of the way these major professional bodies, the UKCC, ENB and CCETSW, have incorporated experiential learning within their official policies. The other half of the story comes from the harder-edged professions, exemplified by engineering. For intending and practising engineers the key factor is membership and registration. Registration follows a recommendation from one of the engineering institutions to the Engineering Council, which holds the register. Recommendations will only be made when a candidate has completed a course in engineering in a university or college which has been approved specifically by a board of moderators in that particular engineering institution or has applied successfully for membership later. Experiential learning thus raises a crucial issue.

At one level the question is, will an engineering institution recognize for membership purposes a degree programme in engineering which includes the possibility of any form of experiential learning standing as the equivalent to part of an approved course? If the answer to that question is yes (and at present it is yes, perhaps or yes, possibly), it will be yes, provided the amount of credit allowed is no more than one year of the total course. Then the next stage is for the university or college offering that engineering degree to seek approval in advance from the engineering institution for that provision. But what if an applicant for an engineering degree brings knowledge and skill which is clearly acceptable to the higher education institution for academic credit but does not equate literally with the content of a part of the course? How then could registration be granted? So far the answer is that it could not.

At this level experiential learning and its assessment are highlighting the tension between academic institutions and the various engineering institutions over the curriculum for engineering courses. And 'curriculum' does not refer merely to content. There are fundamental pedagogical and general education factors involved as well. At present there is no easy solution to these questions. In time a solution must be found. Engineering cannot stand apart for long from the general acceptance by all kinds of bodies that learning can merit recognition wherever and however it occurs.

NCVQ may be an important influence in effecting this change. Led by the Chartered Institute of Builders, which comes under the umbrella of the Engineering Council, there are moves to produce NVQs at levels 4 and 5 which overlap with graduate and postgraduate qualifications. Since levels 4 and 5 are being devised by Industry Lead Bodies composed of employers, the engineering institutions are bound to be affected. APEL is a required route for seeking the award of an NVQ. It could be, therefore, that the engineering profession will need to reconsider its stance on APEL.

Experiential learning in relation to the licence to practise, the next level, is both more and less complicated. Professional recognition does not necessarily carry with it a licence to practise in the sense that without professional membership practice is illegal. The case for nursing and social work is settled. So is it for teachers. For lawyers and doctors too. But for engineers membership of a professional body is only a legal requirement for those working in nuclear safety, and mining and reservoir construction. However, though lack of membership may have no bearing on an individual's right to be employed it can affect seriously their ability to obtain employment itself. Being able to cite professional membership as well as an engineering degree on application forms, either for a first appointment or in mid-career, is bound to be a considerable advantage. So pressure could well be experienced by engineering institutions from a third direction, individuals as well as higher education and NCVQ.

All of this was thrown into a completely different context by the government's decision to scrap the CNAA, to provide for the incorporation of polytechnics as universities and the movement of some Colleges of Higher Education direct to university status. The result of this is there are now some 100-plus academic institutions with the authority to use APEL in any of the ways so far mentioned in collaboration with professional bodies.

Confronted by these developments the newly formed Higher Education Quality Council has promoted a National CATS Development Project with the task of formulating ways that the use of credit accumulation can be extended, now that there is no overarching body responsible for the academic standards in over half of the higher education institutions. Part of that project concerns the Validity and Credibility of Off-Campus Learning, which incorporates APEL. Its inquiries led to extensive consultative meetings with over 50 professional bodies. It appeared that many were anxious that differences in the credit ratings of their courses by different universities could lead to variations in academic standards. In the absence of CNAA's CATS Registry some were making direct arrangements with an individual university or a group of universities. Some were already making academic transfer arrangements from one professional body to another. All wanted a clarification about the relationship between NCVQ's levels 4 and 5 and higher education. Most lamented the demise of CNAA and wanted the establishment of a national forum so that employers, professional bodies with NCVQ, and higher education could consider these matters. APEL will run through all of them. In many ways, therefore, for many of the professions experiential learning is at the same stage as it was for higher education at the beginning of the 1980s but in a far more uncertain context. As things settle down, in time it is bound to gain the same acceptance.

7

APEL and Teacher Training

So far APEL has not featured much in initial teacher training; yet it is almost bound to do so simply because of the alterations announced by successive Secretaries of State to the regulations governing the initial training of teachers. In 1992 the Department for Education (DFE) announced that in future students in training for teaching should spend 80 per cent of their time in schools. That figure was reduced later in 1992 by the next Secretary of State to 66.66 per cent. Essentially this requirement relates to school-centred training, which is quite different from school-based secondary training. The latter has been developed systematically over the last twenty years by universities and colleges offering teacher training courses, and was a condition for accreditation as set out in Circular 9/92.

These new arrangements for the school-centred initial training of teachers are being taken further through another Education Bill, introduced in November 1993, which will establish a new body called the Teacher Training Agency (TTA), replacing the Council for the Accreditation of Teacher Education. In England TTA will take over the funding of teacher training, including research, from the Higher Education Funding Council (HEFC), so separating teacher education from the rest of higher education provision. In Wales the HEFC retains its financial responsibility. Individual schools or consortia of schools are to be authorized to offer initial teacher training courses. The TTA will have the power to fund individual schools or consortia of schools for conducting school-centred teacher training programmes which have been duly approved by that body, and will ensure an appropriate balance between teacher training courses offered on a school-centred basis and those offered by higher education institutions. Members of the TTA will be appointed by the Secretary of State. As has been the case with successive Education Acts, the Secretary of State proposes to assume an even wider range of powers than before over teacher training. Whatever the merits of the latest alterations, if they are going to be effective they ought to involve systematic use of the assessment of experiential learning.

Half-way through 1993 there was a flurry of suggestions from the DFE about various ways of enabling older men and women to achieve Qualified Teacher Status after completing courses which were much shorter than the four-year Bachelor of Education degree or the one-year post-graduate certificate plus a first degree. A proposed one-year course brought a derisive cry of 'Mum's Army', an entirely unjustified reaction to what was suggested. That course was and remains an unlikely runner; but the search for a considerably shortened one continues. Given the use in higher education of APEL and credit accumulation there seems to be no intrinsic problem in awarding credit towards the academic part of the course. Some teacher training courses already operate in that way. But so far no acceptable solution has been agreed about ways of giving formal recognition for the practical skills of teaching which might have been acquired through working with children or young people in other contexts than school. APEL is connected with all these actual and potential developments.

The newest initiative in these matters is a proposal by the Secretary of State that there should be a new category of people, Specialist Teaching Assistants, working with young children in primary schools. The details have yet to be worked out, but the idea is to upgrade the skills of successful voluntary and paid classroom assistants in schools so that they can work with small groups of children in support of fully-qualified teachers. Again, it is difficult to see how APEL can fail to feature in any course designed to certify Specialist Teaching Assistants, who have already had successful school experience as ancillaries or volunteers.

However, APEL for experienced teachers on In-Service Education and Training for Teachers (INSET) post-qualifying courses has made some headway since the mid-1980s, albeit through the back door. Responding to the CATS regulations introduced in 1986, some polytechnics began to develop arrangements whereby teachers who had undertaken in-service courses provided by their local education authorities could claim academic credit towards a further qualification. In a way this was prior learning coming into play under the experiential banner. But so far this is not a widespread provision, and as a facility it is certainly not well known among teachers.

APEL has also entered the world of experienced teachers in schools and further education through the front door, via Essex Institute of Higher Education, now renamed Anglia Polytechnic University. The admission tutor for a master's degree in Education faced a difficult problem: the regulations for the course restricted entry to teachers holding a bachelor's degree. Some of the early applicants did not hold one, but were clearly very experienced and knowledgeable and, as far as the admission tutor could judge, were as well able to cope with the course as some graduates. This most unsatisfactory state of affairs was resolved after lengthy negotiations through recourse to APEL. Those applicants without a first degree were given the opportunity of taking a short intensive course during which they would go through the APEL procedures, and then submit a substantial piece of work which related directly to their teaching experience and demonstrated a firm grasp of the theory underlying whatever topic they had chosen to write about. This piece of work was then assessed by internal and external examiners and a pass was taken as evidence of having completed satisfactorily the equivalent to the B Ed thesis. Thus, while such applicants did not hold a first degree in education, they proved that they had reached the required standard as a result of their teaching experience, their reading and in-service courses. The principle was established: APEL for serving teachers is acceptable, always provided that the evidence of learning is convincing.

The role of APEL in initial teacher training has not been explored in the same systematic way, but it seems almost inevitable that it will have to be, given the changes in regulation for initial training already announced, the amount of time student teachers are now to spend in schools, and the further changes which it appears the Secretary of State has in mind. Spending time in schools so as to reach the standards necessary to attain a degree or a post-graduate certificate in education and reach qualified status as a teacher, means learning as much from time spent in school as formerly was learned from the teaching given in college or university. Indeed, the assumption in the minds of those who have made these new regulations is that trainee teachers will learn *more* and learn to be better professional teachers from time in school than they would in teacher training departments. This is mere assertion; there is no empirical evidence to support it. But that is what the new arrangements imply.

It follows that a very considerable additional load is being put on schools and their teaching staff, and, what is not always realized, on the validating universities and colleges which will have the responsibility of awarding degrees and post-graduate certificates under the requirements which they have to meet for academic audit.

One way of trying to tackle this new situation is to use the APEL techniques already tried and tested in other fields and then incorporate them in learning agreements. Schools are exceptionally busy places. The best laid plans are always liable to be interrupted and only the unpredictable is predictable. Teaching and learning is a messy, indeterminate, often intimidating and inscrutable business. So if trainee teachers are going to be able to learn theory as well as practice from their longer time in schools then two things are essential. They must be equipped with a sensible learning plan to give them a sense of security in what they are supposed to be learning. They must be enabled to learn from their experience.

Learning from experience for trainee teachers is APEL by a different name in a different place. In other spheres of employment it has increasingly come to be accepted that work-based learning is only significant when it is intentional. That means taking steps to see that it is intentional. In turn that means planning and negotiating what seems to be a sensible plan for learning in the particular circumstances in which the individual is going to be working. So it will have to be for trainee teachers. Given the differences between schools, the differences between classes in the same school, the differences between teaching, say, English Literature and teaching Craft & Design Technology, there are bound to be elements in what trainee teachers can learn which are common to all of them in any one school, as well as elements which are significantly different when one trainee's assignment is compared with another. This, despite the fact that each trainee is spending the same amount of time in the school-based part of the course. This is no easy task. Only experienced teachers will be able to identify both the common and the particular elements as 'learning intentions' which go into the 'learning plan' and are turned into a formal Learning Agreement.

Trainee teachers will need guidance as to what can be learned from experience. That experience is not confined to the classroom where the trainee teacher actually does some practice teaching. It needs to include observing skilled teachers at work, registering the different relationships that are on display in the staff room, trying to understand the principles on which the head seems to work and the education philosophy underlying them, as well as learning about the large and small change of managing curriculum issues. In other words, the trainee teacher has to be helped to learn about the school as a whole, including the growth and development of its pupils, and not just how to prepare and conduct lessons.

For a trainee teacher to be able to cover that range of learning as the content of a professional course leading to the status of qualified teacher requires a good deal of time for systematic reflection. It will also require considerable time to extract and record in clear statements what has been learned from that experience. So much of what happens in schools is more or less on the wing. Without subsequent thought it is likely to be lost or, more probably, just ignored. Yet it may be highly significant for both theory and practice. There is also going to be a need for some means of relating things which have been so learned from practice to some theoretical framework and thus providing coherence. And the end point of all of this for the trainee teacher is that there needs to be a secure way of producing evidence for the assessments which will have to be made of what has been learned. Notebooks and diaries will not be enough. So the trainee teacher needs to become a student going through APEL procedures.

Trainee teachers cannot possibly cope with the proposed school-based course without consistent advice, help and support. Experienced teachers are the only people qualified to give it, and doing so will place excessive demands on them. A teacher/supervisor will have to size up the capabilities of the trainee teacher, and the possibilities which the school can offer to that trainee for learning about the theory as well as the practice of doing the teacher's job.

He or she will need to agree an overall learning programme with the trainee and then settle ways of monitoring the latter's progress along those agreed lines in such a way that reliable assessments can be made. They must be reliable to meet the necessary standards for inclusion in the final results for the degree or post-graduate certificate: the licence to practise in teaching depends on it. By definition, if things are left loose and to chance, then not only will the trainee's learning be undisciplined and erratic, but any assessments are liable to be invalid. Furthermore, it is the university which awards the degree or post-graduate certificate, and the trainee teacher's achievements on the school-based element of the overall programme are subject to the scrutiny not only of that awarding body, but also of the external agencies that are responsible for ensuring the quality of what goes on in universities. Learning agreements signed by the trainee teacher, the teacher mentor and perhaps by a tutor from the awarding university or college would be an appropriate way of meeting all those requirements.

Academic audits and academic assessment are now vital concerns for higher education. Any awarding institution working in partnership with schools under the proposed arrangements for initial teacher training will itself need to be thoroughly versed in the principles and procedures of APEL. In some ways they are bound to be advisers, since they alone can make the awards leading to qualified teacher status. And that could be a delicate matter. It is likely to be even more complicated if schools respond to the invitation from the Secretary of State to form consortia and submit proposals to conduct the entire training programme by themselves. Standards will remain the responsibility of the university or college willing to act as the validating authority for any such consortia. So a familiarity with APEL could be a necessity if students in training, their schoolteacher mentors and the qualification-awarding body are to provide the service which these new regulations are expected to provide.

But concern about standards runs wider than the quality of a particular teacher training programme based on a partnership between one or more schools and a validating university or college. Academic audits conducted by the Higher Education Quality Council will look to those wider concerns. But HMIs ought to be able to help ensure that nationwide the standards for teacher education programmes are acceptable. An HMI assigned to work with a group of schools in any one area is in a position to make comments on the quality of the components of the teacher training programme being offered in those schools and at the same time is able to see things from the other end at the university or college acting as the academic partner to those schools. HMIs too, in that case, would need to become well versed in the principles and procedures for APEL.

Given the demise of CNAA, it looks as if a combination of HMI reports and the published results of academic audits are the best means to hand of keeping standards of teacher training programmes under regular review.

Most recently and contentiously, the Secretary of State is proposing to allow consortia of schools to assume responsibility for awarding initial teacher qualifications under the overall authority of the TTA. If successful, this could exclude universities from awarding those qualifications. Questions of academic and professional standards would be even more problematic. The requirements for meeting and securing them would be the same; the mechanisms would change. APEL would remain a factor to be ignored at peril. Learning from experience lies at the heart of these requirements. Unless what the trainees learn is documented thoroughly both trainee and experienced teacher are going to be in difficulties. So, as in other spheres, staff development for the experienced teachers who are going to help the trainees learn is a top priority. This means no more and no less than enabling the experienced teachers to go through the procedures for the assessment of prior experiential learning themselves, as a preparation for enabling their trainees to do the same thing. It also means that they need to understand the ins and outs of negotiating learning agreements, including the complicated business of working out reliable and acceptable assessment procedures.

Many if not most schools now have long experience of working in close collaboration with education departments in universities and colleges of higher education. There is nothing new in the idea of involving schools closely in teacher training and taking considerable responsibility for it as well. For decades many universities and colleges have done this deliberately as part of their normal practice and as a matter of principle. So where schools are working with education departments to comply with the new requirements, they have a resource available, if they wish to use it, for the preparation of their experienced teachers to address this new situation. The quality of teachers in the future depends on getting things right.

Through APEL all these questions have been faced and dealt with in other spheres of activity. There is plenty of help at hand for those who want it, if they have understood just how important APEL is in the new arrangements for preparing trainees for teaching in schools.

APEL and an administrative change could go a long way to solving the problem referred to earlier of enabling men and women to receive formal recognition, and therefore credit, towards their teaching qualification for practical teaching skills which they acquired while not working in schools. Take any successful nursery nurse with an NNEB qualification or an unqualified, experienced and successful youth worker. Using the systematic reflection on experience techniques of APEL, they could be enabled to give an account of the theoretical basis of any teaching they undertook as a trainee teacher in schools. By observing their capacity to enable pupils to learn in classrooms a skilled assessor could readily make a judgement about their having reached the required standards. If both forms of evaluation produced evidence that they had reached the levels required for a final assessment there would seem no good reason for not saying so officially. In effect, this is asserting that experienced people such as the NNEB qualification-holder or the youth worker ought to be able to qualify when they merit it rather than having to wait until the course is officially over. This is arguing for differential completion speeds.

These arrangements would be possible only if there was an administrative change to the regulations governing the funding of initial teacher training and the administration of students' grants and maintenance. But surely this would be a small price to pay for effecting the reform that the DFE would like to introduce, especially since it would save taxpayers' money and trainee teachers' time.

8

APEL, Employment and Unemployment

The assessment of prior experiential learning is significant for employment because of its connection with training, retraining and skill enhancement. APEL can contribute to meeting the pressing need, however the need is expressed, for the country to lift the general level of education and training in the whole workforce. It can also help point up strategic issues for companies, at all levels of operation. It is not just a question of making sure that those men and women who actually provide services can keep up with the technological changes that continually change the way they work, but also of keeping organizers and managers up to the mark. Whether in the production industry, or in the vast range of service industries, the same applies, as it does in the professions – medical, social work, the law; the list is endless. In every case, because of the scale of the task, keeping up-to-date is only possible if people go on learning while they are working, through their day-to-day work. So far most of the further training available has been tuned to the needs of middle and upper management. Far too little attention has been paid to the training needs of the vast numbers of employees who produce the goods and services the country requires.

APEL can contribute in three fundamental areas: determining the starting point for training programmes; providing recognition of skills and motivation, and coping with large numbers of trainees. Any post-experience programme of personal and occupational development will succeed to the extent that the programme begins where the participants actually are. The problem is that too often the very experienced people who provide courses for post-experience development make inappropriate assumptions about this. In fact, there is no means of their estimating where course participants are because any group of experienced people, at any level, bring with them not only their own accumulated store of knowledge and skill and their own personal intentions but also a brief from their employer as to what they are expected to get out of the course or learning programme. No matter how carefully the course or programme provider has done homework on where they expect the course participants to be, the only way of being accurate is to find out. That takes the business directly into APEL. And whether it is for externally provided programmes or internal courses of up-dating and retraining, the same applies: APEL offers a way of identifying the most helpful starting point for retraining, skill enhancement and progression.

The position of people in employment is no different from the position of many people returning to study in formal education. Many of them have acquired knowledge and skills of which they are unaware because they take them for granted. Recognition of what they have learned can establish the ground floor for future accumulation of knowledge. Once they have a sense of being recognized for what they have learned already, people find that learning more seems an inviting possibility. Motivation is fuelled, strengthened and there to be tapped. So often people who are quite capable of learning more are scared of the idea. Perhaps their school experience was discouraging. Perhaps they feel overshadowed by other people who work around them, or by friends and relations. Perhaps they feel daunted by the prospect of studying because they assume that it means giving up precious time at home and attending classes in uncongenial places, or because the prospect seems too wearying, given all the other things there are to do in their own time. APEL can help deal with most of those apparent obstacles.

The scale of the task of lifting the general level of performance throughout employment is vast, yet there is no chance of releasing large numbers from their work to attend retraining courses elsewhere. Financially it is impossible, save for a few. It is often seen as undesirable too, a potential waste of time and money. For smaller, even medium-sized, businesses, sending people away on courses is not only impossible financially, it would disrupt established work routines in which everyone knows their job and there are no substitutes on the payroll. Thus learning in the workplace provides the only possible solution, and APEL can be the trigger for this.

There are a number of ways in which APEL can be put to use for retraining and development within companies. Employers can collaborate in various ways with further and higher education institutions over retraining and up-dating. And the Employee Development Programme approach provides channels which are ripe for development.

Like other developments mentioned already, APEL first entered the sphere of employment in any systematic way after 1986, when the Credit and Accumulation Transfer Scheme and Registry were established in the Council for National Academic Awards. Everyone concerned was surprised at the speed with which some major employers recognized the opportunity which CATS offered them. For the first time in Britain on a systematic basis it became possible for the in-house education and training programmes of an employer to be considered for the award of academic credit at both bachelor's and master's degree levels. It meant having those courses and programmes scrutinized by academics in the relevant discipline to determine whether their content deserved consideration as the equivalent of a component in a higher education course. That done, it was necessary to determine the size of the component taken as a proportion of a full-time student's study programme, and to make an academic judgement about the level of the component, measured again against the requirements of formal taught courses in the academic institution (Dearden, 1991a).

The nub of these negotiations was assessment. Most employers were not particularly concerned to adopt the forms of assessment required in higher education. Their in-house programmes of retraining and development were provided according to the company's needs, and the only form of assessment they were interested in related to the ability of their employees to perform their duties more effectively. Some way had to be found of meeting both employers' and academics' requirements, and that meant some accommodation on both sides. It emerged, however, that both would benefit from that accommodation: the employers realized that their own courses could be improved by paying closer attention to course content in relation to the performance of participants, and they saw how that performance could be judged rigorously. And the academics realized that the courses they offered internally to their traditional students could be improved through incorporating material which was up-to-date and in line with what employers looked for when they were recruiting graduates. The success of this development can be gauged by the fact that at the time of writing there are some 50 firms and professional bodies which have used this facility for having their own courses scrutinized as contributing to higher education courses.

All of this took place under the heading of APEL. This was knowledge and skill acquired without reference to educational institutions and was uncertificated as such. The thrust of this collaboration between employers and academics was to turn it into certificated learning. And there were two important spin-offs: public recognition that some employers were providing education and training courses which had the academic status of higher education provision, and direct involvement for the first time of employers in the assessment of academic learning. The latter development has particular significance (Dearden, 1991b), as will emerge later (p. 58).

Through the establishment of the CATS Registry at CNAA learning agreements for full-time employees became a possibility. If academic credit could be gained through APEL based on companies' in-house courses on a credit accumulation basis, there was no reason why academic credit could not be awarded on the basis of negotiated learning programmes for individuals, provided that academic requirements were met. The successful operation of learning agreements again involved some important developments. The first was that negotiations had to include not only the prospective learner (an employee) and an academic to ensure that what was being proposed as a future learning programme was acceptable in academic terms, but also had to involve the employer to make sure that what the employee was going to learn was consistent with the way the employer foresaw the company's future needs. And that meant trying to base the negotiated programme on the existing work of the employee. Being a negotiated arrangement it followed that it could be renegotiated. The employee's work assignments or even his/her position within the company might change and it was only common sense to be prepared to take account of any such changes. This nailed learning agreements as part of the company's own training and education programme.

A second development connected with learning agreements was that the results of any credit rated company in-house courses could be incorporated within the agreements. And a third was that any on-the-job learning (APEL) that was relevant to the qualification being sought could also be included, and could be acceptable academically when it had been assessed.

A fourth development was hardly new: it was an existing phenomenon the significance of which was highlighted through APEL. It was demonstrated that the success of an employee in this kind of learning programme depends very largely on the support given by the line manager or supervisor. This was emphasized in the pilot project for learning agreements (1987–88) run with Jaguar Cars, Wimpey Food International, JBS Computers and the Manpower Services Commission. There was a clear correlation between the support and encouragement provided by supervisors and the progress of the employees and their eventual results (Dearden, 1989).

Employer involvement in assessment, already touched upon, was a fifth development. It was pragmatically necessary involvement as well as being a matter of principle. The principle was that if the employer helped to determine what the employee would learn at higher education level, and the entire undertaking was a contribution to overall training needs, then the employer needed to have confidence in the operation and thus be a witness of the completion stage. The pragmatic necessity for employer involvement was that because some of the additional learning to be undertaken could result in the employee producing documents or artefacts which related directly to the company's work, it would have been inappropriate at best and objectionable at worst for assessments to be conducted solely by academics.

The last development was that academic staff were supervising the academic work of employees/students and being ultimately responsible for it, when none of those students needed to come anywhere near the academic institution itself.

In summary, then, learning agreements demonstrated that together many employers and their employees had to hand three potential sources of academic credit towards either a bachelor's or a master's degree and did not know it. Furthermore, it was shown that the entire retraining and up-dating exercise could be conducted without employees leaving the premises.

The success of the first pilot scheme led the Department of Employment's Training, Enterprise and Education Directorate to fund four further projects of a similar kind and a number of others which use many of the principles established, all as part of a general policy initiative to develop further collaboration between employers and education at higher education level. And at the heart of TEED's overall programme there is the search for schemes of assessment in which employers play a significant academic role. None of this would have been possible without the acceptance of APEL as a valid and reliable way of assessing learning acquired without necessary reference to academic institutions. As such APEL is a significant matter for employers as they grapple with their retraining needs.

The form of APEL-based collaboration between employers and higher education just described can be extended into major activities. Learning agreements and credit rating of companies' courses can lead to tailormade provision: when company and higher education institution have come to trust one another and can jointly formulate degree programmes which in their entirety meet both the employer's need for programmes which will increase the capabilities of his workforce and the academic's need for a course which meets acceptable academic criteria. This major stage can lead on to an employing organization becoming recognized and accredited in its own right not only for teaching courses at higher education level but for making its own academic awards. This has long been the practice in the USA, where several top companies have that status. In this country so far only British Telecom has been accredited as an academic institution, but no doubt in time more will follow.

At a different level further education can collaborate with employing organizations in much the same way. The newest way in which APEL comes into the picture for employment is through the vocational qualifications established by the National Council for Vocational Qualifications. This has been a huge and costly initiative funded by government to establish occupational competences at five different levels for every occupation in the land. Each competency is described together with the criteria which have to be met before an individual can be awarded the competency certificate. Each is a stand-alone competency, meaning that there are no prescribed courses which have to be taken before an individual can ask for assessment. And since many employees have gone a long way towards meeting some of the criteria for a competence, and some employers see the NVQ system as a good way of encouraging their workforce to improve their skills, two other matters have to be settled; assessment and top-up facilities. Much of the assessment is done within and by the company itself under the heading of work-based assessment; APEL by another name. But when a company does not wish to go down that route it may well turn to a college of further education. It may also turn to a college for help with the top-up requirement. The problem is this. How best can an employee who has demonstrated an ability to meet some of the criteria for a particular competence, acquire the skill, knowledge and understanding necessary to meet those criteria which have not yet been met? The answer is often that a further education college can provide the necessary help. And as with the schemes described for higher education, APEL plays a vital part at every stage of the procedures involving vocational qualifications.

Within a company, APEL can be every bit as significant. It can only be so, however, when a company has accepted the logic of saying that training and retraining begins at home in the workplace. The corollary to that first logical step is to recognize that learning at the workplace will only become an everyday occurrence if ways and means are found to see that it is intentional. And this means finding ways of extending explicitly the responsibilities of line managers and supervisors so that they become mentors and coaches to those who answer to them. This is the target for companies if prosperity is to return to the country, and it is also one of the criteria for judging how far a company is a learning organization. The responsibility for encouraging employees to learn must be seen as part of the day-to-day work of the line manager, and not the sole preserve of a special training department.

This is where within employment APEL really comes into its own. If a line manager or supervisor wants to know how best to meet the training needs of his group of people, he first needs to find out where they are. The process involved may be a skills audit, or a training needs analysis; it may be related to staff appraisal systems; it may be part and parcel of something closely related to the idea of a Record of Achievement. Whatever it is, it means having available some set of procedures and support materials or guideline documents to take the general idea forward.

Just as any development of APEL which involves staff in education institutions requires some programme of professional development beforehand to prepare the staff properly for what they are expected to do, so too within employment the satisfactory use of APEL means that line managers and supervisors need proper preparation. Like the other schemes described so far, this preparatory process has been tried and tested – in three GEC companies. Managers spent a long time working with a professional experienced in APEL, to work out from their own experience what steps would need to be taken for them to adopt as part of their role, mentoring or coaching. They were extracting from their experience as managers and supervisors the key things they would have to include in any document aimed at helping their colleagues with comparable responsibilities, and at the same time they were making their own guidelines for coaching. That was stage one. Stage two was using the documents and doing the work for real with some of their employees.

The scheme worked very well. And it worked well because it exposed a strategic issue: almost the first thing to emerge from the exploration stage was that there was little point in line managers trying to act as coaches if their superiors did not fully support the enterprise. They too needed to have some sense of acting as coaches towards others. This resulted, in one case, in training budgets being devolved to line managers so that the activities could be properly resourced. In another case the materials developed were used to link the employees' performance at work with a skills requirements analysis which the company worked out for itself. In another case the APEL route was used for a direct connection with a learning agreement which took the individual towards an honours degree in engineering. And when the Avon Authority's guidance unit was introduced to the materials, they adopted them forthwith as a means of promoting their own programme for linking the development of their guidance officers to the training standards evolved by the Training Lead Body.

As one training manager put it, introducing the idea of APEL to his company worked as a catalyst for a whole range of things which related to training, as well as providing a cohering influence. So for any internal arrangements companies may make for training and retraining, APEL can be a powerful influence (Braham, 1993).

There is a completely different way of thinking about APEL in relation to training within employment, and that is in connection with schemes such as Ford UK's Employee Development and Assistance Programme (EDAP). As with similar programmes in Lucas, Rover, and Peugeot Talbot, the intention is to encourage employees to become or continue to be active learners through making money available for them to study. But the distinguishing factor of Ford's EDAP programme in the context of this discussion is that EDAP is quite separate from Ford's own in-house training programmes. This is explicit, and the way the programme actually works shows what it means in practice. Employees have to make formal application to their local plant EDAP committee for financial support for what it is they wish to do under the programme. Any application which looks as if it relates to something which the committee considers to be the responsibility of the company's own training department gets rejected.

Thus with the Ford EDAP programme the APEL aspect comes in not in any formal sense; it is implicit. Any Ford employee making an application under EDAP has to have thought about what it is that she or he wants to learn about and why. That is bound to be the case, whether it is bricklaying, learning to drive, studying a foreign language or something to do with information technology. And they can only have done that by thinking about both their past and their future. If the process were made explicit, it would be systematic reflection on experience. But simply because it is not made explicit, that does not mean it doesn't happen. Countless Ford employees have progressed from relatively lowly learning activities to serious study in further and higher education. Where APEL is explicit the results are impressive. There are about 100 Ford workers from the Halewood plant near Liverpool who have used their experiential learning for admission to a first degree offered by the Liverpool Institute of Higher Education or for credit towards that degree. There are now hundreds more on degree programmes offered in collaboration with Anglia Polytechnic University.

Of course there is a sense in which APEL within Ford UK's EDAP, which stands quite outside Ford's formal training programme, can hardly be seen as making a contribution to the employer's preoccupation with training and retraining. However, there is a case for saying that it does. Whatever other motives the unions and management may have had when they first negotiated the EDAP scheme, they were acknowledging that employees who learn are better employees than those who do not. That in itself connects with whatever training the company requires for its own purposes, because it is tapping the motivation of individuals to learn. And since that motivation to learn has been born out of their own interests, it means that they are much more likely to undertake the company's training more purposefully. In other words, what they are encouraged to do with their own time is likely to have influence on what they do with the company's time.

Partially influenced by the success of many employees using their experiential learning for progression onto formal study in further and higher education, Ford have now embarked on a scheme for upgrading hundreds of their engineers, using APEL as the foundation for that programme. All this represents another dimension of the ways that APEL can serve the urgent need for upgrading the skills of the workforce.

Influenced largely by the success of employee development programmes adopted by major employers, efforts have been made to promote similar schemes for smaller, medium-sized businesses. Kent TEC successfully launched a scheme involving some ten medium-sized businesses in East Kent. So have the Heart of England TEC and other organizations (NIACE, 1994). Again tacitly, APEL comes into play. As soon as employees are given the chance to choose what it is they wish to learn about, then they are reflecting on their previous experience as the basis for determining their learning intentions.

'Investors in People' is a joint CBI/government initiative, once more intended to encourage employers to take the training of their employees more seriously. To achieve the insignia of an Investor in People an organization has to show that it has met a long list of criteria:

An Investor in People makes a public commitment from the top to develop all employees to achieve the business objectives.

An Investor in People regularly reviews the training and development needs of all employees.

An Investor in People takes action to train and develop individuals on recruitment and throughout their employment.

An Investor in People evaluates the investment in training and development to assess achievement and improve future effectiveness.

Since most of the effort implied by those requirements for becoming an Investor in People has to be undertaken within employing organizations, the role of APEL is clear: it can offer a way of conducting a skill and knowledge audit as the base line for the further training and development of individuals. Doing that is likely to increase their motivation and interest in further training. Because of the need to undertake much of the training and development in house, APEL provides a way of monitoring what individuals are actually accomplishing. And if there is any interest in relating those achievements to formal qualifications, the APEL record provides a readymade way of doing so.

Few people would dispute the importance of the phrase 'from the top' in the first statement about Investors in People. This is the key to effective training and development. APEL can make a contribution here as well. Since training and development is an issue for employers, then it should be clear that APEL is a live issue for them as well.

When the focus switches from employment to unemployment the tune is different but the motifs are the same. Some are intensified. It is well nigh impossible for those fortunate ones who have not suffered unemployment to get inside the mind of someone unemployed. So many complicated reactions come into play; there is the loss of status, which leads to awkwardness, if not embarrassment, with friends, relations, acquaintances and − not least − with children who go off to school and have to face their peers; the loss of the social context of work − meeting people, the rhythm of going to and returning from work with its counterpart in the rhythms of domestic life; the demeaning business of filling in forms at the Social Security Office, and the wretchedness of queuing for benefits, and the inevitable financial worries. There are the hopes, disappointments and fears about finding another job, and the relentlessness of going on looking. All these factors are enough to demoralize anyone who is unemployed, and for those who experience them for a long time the effect is bound to be debilitating.

In the present economic circumstances there is little point in talking airily about retraining, with the usual rhetoric about everyone needing to change their careers several times during a lifetime in the future, true though that is. The unemployment figures are so large and frightening that retraining courses risk preparing people for jobs which do not exist. So the initial need is to devise ways of helping people in their wretchedness retain some sense of their own worth, or rebuild it, or even create it, since many unemployed have never been encouraged to think of themselves as worth much at all, apart from the wages they managed to earn. And this is where APEL can be significantly relevant for the unemployed.

All the points made about people wanting to study more, about those in employment needing to extend their knowledge and skills to keep abreast of the demands made on them at work, hold true for the unemployed. Capabilities taken for granted, knowledge and skill stored away and ignored because no-one ever said it was of any significance, because no-one was sufficiently interested to find out what it was, all that can be of huge significance for the unemployed if only they can be brought to recognize it. And that is the key: how to enable people to come to that realization. It takes time, trying to scan experience and spot what has been learned from it, and it is likely to take a great deal more time for someone suffering the lowered morale of being without a job than for any of the other categories of people for whom APEL can be a boon.

Most of the government's initiatives for the unemployed have made a token gesture towards restoring morale through self-assessment. Since 1979 there have been twenty-two successive programmes related to the unemployed, but the trouble with those which purported to involve some form of self-assessment was that the time allowed was utterly inadequate. The contractual terms under which the Employment Department released funding to the providers of programmes for the unemployed prevented the allocation of sufficient time to individuals at the beginning of any programme to create the best chance of making a success of the available training. And to a large extent that is why so many training courses have failed. Many people trying to come to terms with the personal problems of being unemployed are in no condition to produce within a few days an action plan for their future work, no matter how much information is available about the range of training opportunities waiting to be used. Yet that was the way programmes for the unemployed were supposed to work. There was no time to pick up the pieces of a ruptured life, to get a different set of bearings on the world in which some future had to be constructed.

Furthermore, because all the programmes had to be related to vocational skill and training a whole range of opportunities for getting the unemployed back to work was missed. Lending a hand with a community newsletter, whether writing for it, raising money for it, producing it or distributing it, can be a more effective way of helping some people to develop ideas for their future employment, than following any kind of formal course (McGiney, 1993). Learning more about geography, history or biology can be a better way of preparing to undertake a training course in information technology than being jumped into it straight away as a beginner. The most important element for any retraining is motivation, and a mind that is actually working. Anything which gets that mind working is bound to be valuable. This is where APEL can be so effective. It can provide the opportunity for people to recognize what they have accomplished already, even though they had not realized it. The mind is working and likely to be working hard, because the tasks are entirely personal and not imposed from outside. Thinking about the past, all of it, not merely past employment, is a good way of trying to plot the future. And if the mind is working along those lines, someone is more likely to be ready for engaging in training. APEL is indeed a serious matter for the unemployed. Perhaps even more to the point, it is a serious matter for policy-makers (Hunt and Jackson, 1993). So much of the money spent has been wasted; it is time to recognize that some activities which do not relate immediately to an occupational skill can be a better bargain than tunnelled-vision training.

REFERENCES

Braham, Jeff (1993): *Learning for Success.* London: Learning from Experience Trust.

Dearden, Gerald (1989): *Learning while Earning: Learning Contracts for Employees*. London: Learning from Experience Trust.

Dearden, Gerald (1991a): *The Credit Rating of In-Company Courses: How to Get Double Value*. London: Learning from Experience Trust.

Dearden, Gerald (1991b): *The Assessment of Prior Learning: An Introduction for Employers, Employees and Academic Assessors*. London: Learning from Experience Trust.

Hunt, Jenny and Jackson, Heather (1993): *Vocational Education for the Adult Unwaged: Developing a Learning Culture*. London: Kogan Page.

McGiney, Veronica (1992): *Some British and European Findings*. Leicester: NIACE.

NIACE (1994): *Adult Learning*, Vol 5, Number 9: Learning in the Workplace. Leicester: NIACE.

9

Experiential Learning and Its Assessment

The assessment of experiential learning is now part of a wider debate about quality and assessment in higher education, in further education and in connection with National Vocational Qualifications. This context, affected by government legislation and anxiety, if not panic, about the need for vocational qualifications to lift the general skill level of the nation's workforce, is entirely different from that of the early 1980s, when APEL first became part of academic discussion in higher education.

Discussion now runs from questions as to whether the classified honours degree should survive to the problems of attempting to accommodate NVQs and their manner of assessment within higher education's different purposes, taking in such topics as the validity and credibility of off-campus learning (including work-based learning), the role of employers as assessors, the extent to which academic criteria should predominate, and overall questions of quality.

Discussion is conducted in several different but related forums. As incorporated independent chartered institutions, there are now over 100 universities and colleges responsible for the quality of their academic work and the qualifications they award. Each institution now has internal academic audit and quality assurance units to keep their work under continual review. There are over 400 further education colleges which, similarly, have had to develop their own internal procedures for checking the quality of the courses they provide. The Higher Education Funding Council has its own team of quality assessors as a means of collecting additional information to help determine the funds allocated to individual institutions. Similarly, the Further Education Funding Council has its own inspectors, who provide the same function in further education colleges. The Higher Education Quality Council has a Division of Academic Audit to conduct regular visits to institutions to ensure they have the requisite means of assuring the quality of their academic work. National Vocational Qualifications are assessed by specially licensed assessors against criteria laid down by Industry Lead Bodies. The Business and Technology Education Council, City and Guilds and the Royal Society of Arts have their own regulations. Training and Enterprise Councils have their own quality assurance requirements. And since at every level APEL can now feature, it is under continual scrutiny from this wide range of bodies.

All this is dramatically different from the early 1980s when the assessment of prior experiential learning first became a consideration for higher education. Then there were questions about academic assessments of uncertificated learning and about the self-assessment dimension for individuals in APEL. Both led to a series of questions which were not even formulated at the beginning but have proved to be significant for the development of institutions and what they provide. Academic assessments led to a more ready acceptance that learning takes place in many different contexts and often merits formal recognition. Self-assessment led into the wider issue of national provision of education advice and guidance. It was the beginning of what has become an extension of academic authority.

APEL was bound to be a controversial academic issue. Academics were faced with unfamiliar tasks. Instead of considering the results of students who had followed a prescribed syllabus which they and their colleagues had taught, they were asked to make judgements about the quantity, quality and level of claims to knowledge and skill presented by people who had not been their students and who had acquired their learning without any necessary reference to an academic institution.

Inevitably the claims and supporting evidence offered by APEL candidates were unlikely to be the kinds of evidence tutors were in the habit of considering when they assessed the work of their regular students. Instead of essays, laboratory results, projects or artefacts prescribed for students as set assignments, assessors

were confronted by different forms of evidence. A claim to
have learned a section of a business studies or an account-
ancy course might be supported by a dossier of papers written
during employment, a file of correspondence, the accounts taken
from the proceedings of a voluntary body, articles published, or
a list of books studied – in any combination. Someone making a
claim to have mastered part of an information technology course
might have written a computer program and offer that as evidence.
An amateur archaeologist might produce notes and commentary
derived from digs attended as a volunteer or as a paying member
of an expedition. An enthusiastic traveller might present tapes of
conversations in a foreign language, reading lists and an account
of some aspect of a region in a foreign country, outlining its history, economy or art.

What the academic was being asked to do in all those hypo-
thetical cases was to use professional judgement to determine how
far the evidence supported the claim, and whether the claim was
acceptable as the equivalent to conventional requirements. Those
kinds of decisions were and are relatively simple when it is a matter
of considering applications for admission to a course. Admission
tutors have always taken account of the experiential learning of
older applicants for admission, although it was not called that.
Quite apart from anything else it is often a good indication of the
motivation of the applicant for study. And what they are doing
for APEL candidates is in essence no different from what they
are doing with other admission applications: looking for evidence
of an ability to cope with the course. But in these cases the learning
has to be 'quantified'.

For when it comes to considering APEL for admission with
advanced standing, or for academic credit towards an academic
qualification, then all the usual questions need more searching
answers. The issues are:

Authenticity. Is it clear that the material being presented is the
applicant's own work? Any academic can sort that out quickly.

Appropriateness. Does the evidence relate directly to the claim
and does it support it? This is simply applying the standard test
for the validity of any assessment procedure.

Balance between theory and practice. This is more difficult. As a
rough rule of thumb APEL candidates are likely to be practice-rich
and theory-poor. For academic purposes, unless there is evidence

of some understanding of the underlying theory on which the practice is based, then any claim is unacceptable. And the crude test for this is whether the candidate shows any ability to apply the theory in a different and unfamiliar context from the one implied by the practice.

Assuming that the quality of the claim is acceptable, two further decisions have to be made – on *quantity* and *level*. For quantity (the amount of academic credit to be awarded) it is a question of weighing the claim as a proportion of a full-time student's load. And the decision on level involves a professional judgement about where the knowledge and skill being claimed fits into the various stages of the course in question.

At this stage it is worth repeating the cardinal rule for APEL in higher education. Assessments should be conducted by academics who have had no part in helping applicants prepare their claims for submission, nor advising them in any way. This safeguards the integrity of assessment procedures. That integrity is buttressed when two assessors are involved in making the final judgement. However, there is an interesting addendum, which in the long run may prove to be of considerable significance. Experience has shown that assessments made by well-informed generalists correlate closely with those made by subject specialists. This is a matter which will be referred to later.

Two fairly recent developments have made decisions on prior learning easier. One is the modularization of academic courses and the attachment of learning outcomes to course units. The point about modularization is this. Right from the beginning of APEL discussions in higher education it was obvious that partly because the way that adults learn is eclectic, and partly because it is unlikely that any adult would have mastered independently an entire year's study for a single honours degree, if APEL was going to become a reality there needed to be some way of relating learning claims to smaller rather than larger portions of study. It so happened, for a number of other reasons, there was a move in a growing number of institutions towards adopting modularization as the best way of organizing academic programmes to fit the needs of the future. APEL was something of a catalyst for this movement. But the essential point is that modularized courses greatly facilitate the assessment of prior and experiential learning.

So do learning outcomes or intentions. Learning outcomes as a syllabus extension in higher education are not the same thing as the competences developed by the National Council for Vocational Qualifications. The General National Vocational Qualifications currently being developed may well narrow the gap between academic and vocational qualifications once their evolution is more advanced. But at present for higher education learning outcomes or intentions simply means that those who prepare syllabuses supplement the description of the content of the course, and the material to be studied, with statements indicating what a student is expected to know and be able to do when the course is completed. For APEL this means that there is an assessment tool available for ready use. Any claim relating to a course expressed in learning outcome terms can be judged more readily by an academic. Equally, since those learning outcomes are published parts of a course description, the APEL candidate can assess a claim in advance of submitting it, thereby saving time all round.

There are limitations to the role of learning outcomes for APEL. This is because while the central purpose of assessing experiential learning is to enable an individual to reveal whatever knowledge and skill is present yet invisible, adults do not learn according to preordained arrangements of knowledge into subject disciplines. Hence there is the question of specific or general credit. Where a claim relates to a particular course, assessment is an open and shut case, given the caveats mentioned already. Specific credit can be awarded. Where programmes of study include provision for options, subjects or topics which a student can choose to follow alongside the requirements for the particular degree, an APEL claim can be accepted, even though it may be a variation on something in the list of options. Here general credit is being awarded. However, if an APEL claim does not come under either of those provisions, the question arises as to whether it can be recognized formally or not.

Say an amateur historian has read widely in a particular area and convinces an academic that the learning displayed is clearly at a level expected of undergraduates and yet the area does not feature in any module, course or programme offered by the institution. Is the claim allowable or not? This is an issue which goes beyond regulations of courses and degrees. It raises questions about the meaning of academic study and its quality. If the evidence is clear that the conceptual grasp of the material studied is equivalent to that required of regular students, the key question is, on what grounds can the claim be disallowed? If the answer is that regulations do not permit it, then questions arise about the appropriateness of the regulations.

This conundrum points to the limitations of learning outcomes. As a guardian of academic quality as represented by awarding certificates and degrees, an academic institution has the power to put its name to any learning attainment, provided that the integrity of the institution is sustained. This issue extends into complicated realms implicit in the acceptance of APEL. That acceptance means acknowledging the validity of learning acquired in many parts of society and its assessment means that it is fit for inclusion in the recognition of learning attainments by higher education. This is an example of the general point about APEL implicitly leading to an extension of academic authority.

This becomes clear as soon as assessment of experiential learning gets applied to learning in the workplace: work-based learning, as the phrase has become. But before turning to that, and partly because it overlaps with it, we should consider the assessment of experiential learning in further education.

The earliest experience of assessing experiential learning in colleges was in connection with access courses, helping students who had not yet acquired the relevant exam results to enter higher education. Acting in accord with higher education institutions, mainly polytechnics, many FE colleges were evolving ways of associating APEL with their access provision. Assessment was thus a shared responsibility between the two collaborating institutions, and for academic purposes it was the admission tutor who had the last word. But it was a start in further education.

Outside that use of APEL, the arrangements for APEL in colleges were laid down for them by the various examining and awarding bodies such as BTEC, RSA, City and Guilds and Pitmans. Those bodies had tentatively begun to develop guidelines for APEL before the arrival of NCVQ. Once its requirements began to feature for both the awarding bodies and the colleges, then assessment took a different turn. Simultaneously colleges had to cope with guidelines issued by the awarding bodies, the sometimes inconsistent interpretation of those regulations by visiting moderators, and preparations for assessment on demand which is inherent in NCVQ, and with its complement, top-up arrangements for those NVQ candidates who fulfil only some of the requirements for a particular unit of competence.

It emerged fairly quickly that for further education the provision of advice and guidance, the self-assessment strand to APEL, became almost a condition for the successful introduction of schemes intended to help students. Add that to the requirements laid down by NCVQ and the awarding bodies, then for staff in further education assessment became something rather different from what developed in higher education. The principles could be similar. Their application was different.

Quite how different becomes clearer when work-based assessment comes into the picture. And once again the differences between further and higher education are striking. Since NCVQ cannot operate at all without the assessment of prior and experiential learning, and since so much of further education's work is related to vocational preparation, the expense of additional arrangements for assessment meant that assessment in the workplace had to be available. It was impossible to see how further education staff could be funded to cope with the large numbers that NCVQ was set up to serve. Inevitably this restricted the role of further education in assessment of NVQs, with implications for the colleges which are only now being worked out. They can become approved assessment centres. They can contract with employers to do assessments and provide the necessary top-up facilities. Similarly they can contract with TECs in the same way to be training providers for any of the succession of government-funded programmes. But in each case the constraining factor is money: whether the college can afford to do so. This will be resolved only when the FEFC has worked out a funding formula which takes those considerations into account, especially for part-time students.

Compared with that, higher education has autonomy when assessing work-based learning and APEL has shown the way. Whether it is the work experience component of sandwich courses, or the most recent development of work-based learning as an option within three-year non-vocational degrees, or the learning at work which part-time students may wish to offer for credit, academic assessments are now being conducted under institutions' own arrangements for quality assurance. The approach is to use a combination of learning intentions, negotiated between student learner, employer and academic to settle the activities which are likely to provide the opportunities for learning what is proposed, and to set down how the results are going to be assessed. The entire procedure operates only with the approval of the institution's academic standards committee as final authority. In this way work-based learning for academic credit is assured of its academic credibility and integrity.

This is where the employer as assessor becomes so important, in relation to academic work. APEL is based on the assertions that learning is valid wherever it occurs, that its assessment is a proper part of the education enterprise, and much of that extra-institutional learning is acquired by people through their work. Since employers are responsible for that learning it seems appropriate that they should have a stake in determining its value. Put differently, great emphasis is being put on employing organizations becoming learning organizations. At the same time, as was discussed in Chapter 8, it is now commonly recognized that much of the in-house education and training offered by some companies to their employees stands favourable comparison with what is provided in universities, meriting the same recognition. For the formal academic world to resist the prospect of employers assessing their own learners or others who come to them as student learners may be understandable, but in the contemporary world it seems somewhat obscurantist.

Much that seems problematic in this area is resolved when it is clear what it is that is being assessed. Broadly speaking, this falls into three categories. There is the acquisition of additional subject knowledge; the application of subject knowledge; and the range of knowledge and skill related to the operation of day-to-day work in employment. The last has always been present for students engaged in any form of work experience, but has not been articulated in any systematic way. This recording of what has been learned from periods of work experience is becoming increasingly important as a vital part of preparing undergraduates to be immediately employable graduates. In these terms, the employer as academic assessor is becoming an important issue. Quite apart from anything else, the assessor role is an admirable way of encouraging some employers to take seriously the idea of trying to make their own organization a truly learning society.

Many of the problems associated with assessment arise from a search for the nearest thing to objectivity. In the human affairs which constitute the daily activity in education there can be no such thing as absolute objectivity. As far as standards go they have to depend ultimately on the professional judgement of academic staff. So the important thing is how they make those judgements. That is important on two counts: there is the way they judge an individual student's performance in set academic tasks; there is the importance of equity as between one student and another. But, as with objectivity, there can be no absolute guarantee of such equity.

Employers have an additional importance in the overall arena of assessment. Ask any employer what use is made of the highly sophisticated classification of results based on relatively finegrained mark distinctions between one grade and another, and like as not the answer will be − not much. What employers are interested in is a broad indication of where an individual stands along a five-point scale, from wonderful and excellent at one end, through the average, plus or minus, to the just about adequate and the downright inadequate. Some will go further and say that all they are interested in is a threefold classification: outstanding, average and below average. What this means in relation to the assessment of experiential learning is that any attempts to impose the same finegrained mark distinctions commonly made on the basis of essays, projects and the like are misbegotten. And further, that some simplification of the assessment business would benefit everyone involved, not least because the time spent could be more profitably spent in helping students to learn.

APEL can bring two other influences to bear on assessment. Engaging employers as partners in assessment can involve assessments of the affective. When a student on any form of work placement is learning about that employing organization, much of what is learned is about relationships, teamwork, communication, authority, the niceties of group dynamics and, perhaps above all, coping with the unexpected and becoming adaptable. And it is first-hand practical learning. Assuming that all that or part of it has featured in the learning intentions agreed for the work placement period, then assessments must include those matters. Traditionally education has been bad at making any such assessments, sticking more safely to the prowess displayed in mastering abstract material. But now, because in employment these matters are at high premium value, if not of paramount importance, assessment must include some means of registering relevant accomplishments. In a sense this could mean a full circle on APEL, with profiling as a kind of portfolio becoming the central instrument for assessment.

The other influence is the need to ensure that quality is secured for all the credit transfer arrangements which are developing so fast. Unless the assessments of work-based learning are rigorously conducted, the transfer of results from one institution to another will not take place. Were that to happen credit transfer would be a meaningless fiction for individuals and a powerful reason for employers using the facilities of credit transfer would be lost. It must always be the right of a receiving institution to reject or modify the assessments made by another. But there must be a set of agreed procedures which diminish the likelihood of such rejections. To a large and probably increasing extent, the expansion of higher education to become a mass provision is going to depend on institutions having confidence in one another's assessment procedures, and the role of APEL in establishing that confidence can be as unexpected as it is strong.

The reason is this. As APEL is a relative newcomer to the field, there is a natural tendency to assess experiential learning more cautiously and more stringently than traditional courses. So in a rather surprising way APEL can lead to the tightening rather than a relaxing of standards. A considerable amount of work is required of APEL candidates to gain academic credit and it is often more demanding than the work completed by students on formal courses. When academics who teach those regular courses, and are initially sceptical of the validity and appropriateness of APEL, see for themselves as assessors the quality of what is put before them, they are often surprised, even delighted. And since it is the academics who have the sole authority to make academic judgements, there is little chance that APEL will lead to a decline in academic standards. Rather, because they guard those standards jealously, when they incorporate APEL in their responsibilities, nothing is left to chance. Their own reputations depend on it. Peer pressure from their colleagues will ensure it if necessary. So, as it has been for so many aspects of teaching and learning, APEL can be something of a catalyst for developments in academic assessment.

All this becomes even more important because of the concern of many professional bodies for the way that APEL can be put to the service of their members. Following the demise of CNAA many feel that they have no reliable point of reference for the standards being applied by individual universities and colleges when they award academic credit for experiential learning. And now it is up to the universities and colleges themselves to convince the professional bodies that their arrangements for assessing experiential learning are beyond reproach.

There is one other aspect to the assessment of experiential learning: peer group assessments. Given the increased importance placed on use of teamwork and on promoting student-centred learning so that students take increased responsibility for their own learning, and remembering that some of them take part in negotiating their own learning programmes, students are often fairly good critics of their own work. Involving them in the assessments of their own work can become an important part of their general education. They could never have more than an influence on their final results, but there could be positive gain in allowing them to take some responsibility for assessment. Once again, APEL can act as a potent influence on this kind of development.

Oral assessment is an approach to the assessment of experiential learning which has not been developed systematically so far. One documented example occurs in information technology. It appears that the nature of the discipline is such that where a course is constructed in sections, it is possible for experts in the discipline to form reliable judgements about the validity of a claim through questioning a candidate closely. In effect this is a sharp probing exercise which gets to the heart of the business, elucidating whatever is hidden until it is revealed. Given the need to find economical ways of conducting APEL there is an urgent need to explore the possibility of conducting assessments by this kind of interview in other disciplines.

Then there is the generalist approach to the assessment of experiential learning. Frequently in development projects which involve specialist courses such as social work or in negotiated learning agreements, the evidence is that preliminary assessments made by a well-informed widely experienced academic correlate closely with those made by a specialist.

So the assessment of experiential learning is a many-sided

business. Like other aspects of APEL it raises more questions than might be expected at first sight.

FURTHER READING

DOE (1988–): *Competence and Assessment*, Quarterly Journal of the Employment Department's Method Strategy Unit. Various articles from issue 1 (1988) onwards.
See also References for Chapter 10 (p. 88).

10

APEL and Staff Development

The issue of staff development crops up in any discussion on APEL, whether on introducing it, doing it, monitoring it, refining it. There is the need to be prepared for new activities, a continuing need for practitioners to get together and compare notes, to find better ways of persuading others of APEL's validity and increasingly to find the most effective ways of ensuring the quality of the service as part of an institution's overall responsibility.

The first serious attempt in Britain to engage in any staff development for people wanting to be engaged in APEL came about in a quite unexpected way. All the earliest conversations about the very possibility of introducing APEL to Britain were preparatory and rudimentary approaches to staff development. It became a serious issue in 1982 when the small group from Thames Polytechnic and Goldsmiths' College sat down with the Policy Studies Institute and tried to plan and then launch the first formal provision of APEL under the title of Making Experience Count. Many of the issues which have exercised staff since then first cropped up at that time.

But the first systematic approach to staff development came about through an approach from an American Community College. Its president had the idea of having some of his students placed in volunteer activities through Community Service Volunteers, but he needed to find some way of planning what they could reasonably be expected to learn from their volunteering and have that learning evaluated so that as a learning experience the period could count towards the award of their associate degree. This was a service which CSV could not provide and so the president approached the Policy Studies Institute, knowing that work was beginning there on the assessment of experiential learning.

By that time there were a number of people from further, adult and higher education, mainly but not exclusively from the London area, meeting in PSI to discuss APEL matters in general. The obvious way of trying to meet the American request was to find some willing partners from that discussion group. But, having found them, there was the problem of getting them prepared adequately for undertaking the tasks involved. The answer was to have someone from the community college come and run a staff development seminar.

And that was what happened. The vice-president provided a two-day intensive programme for about twelve people, taking them first through the various stages of the principles and practice of assessing experiential learning, then all the various elements involved in arriving at negotiated learning agreements, especially the need for being prepared to renegotiate those agreements, and then to establish the modes of assessment. It was outstandingly successful. And as those twelve people began to try and put into practice with American students on CSV placements what they had learned over four years or so with successive cohorts of American students, and as they moved on to other jobs, they took that influence with them. In a most unlikely way a sort of cascading effect was set in train. That early experience points to the value of being taken through exercises by an expert. It implanted some lessons about good practice which it would be hard to learn in any other way.

The purpose of this account is to emphasize the value of first-hand experience. Another instance is the success of study tours to colleges and universities in the USA. Through close connections established between PSI and the American Council for Adult and Experiential Learning (CAEL), the Kellogg Foundation provided funds to PSI for ten people from British institutions to see for themselves the various ways APEL could be deployed for academic purposes. In the early 1980s, ten visited the USA to experience in a limited way the use that American institutions were making of APEL. The idea was to take people from British institutions on an invitation only basis, choosing those who were either figures concerned with national policy or, and often overlapping with that, were institutional leaders committed to the general thesis of APEL, or were academics working directly with students and thus in a position to develop day-to-day practice. The four or five people in a study tour group came from different institutions. They followed a planned week-long programme involving day or half-day visits to six or seven colleges and universities strung along the east coast between Boston and Washington. The simple purpose was to try to stimulate action back home.

Because of the success of the first programme Kellogg funded an extension for a further ten. That got extended from fully-funded to subsidized study tours. Some 180 men and women have now participated. Most have come from higher education, but a growing number come from further education and there have been some academic administrators and national policy-makers. Almost without exception that relatively large number of people say that the study tours are a first-rate piece of staff development. And it is worth reflecting why that is so.

Naturally there is something rather alluring in the prospect of spending a week in the USA, but all the participants know through the fairly extensive network of previous participants that it is quite a hard-going week. Trying to get the most out of a visit is hard work, but the stimulus is greater than just through the visits. All members of a study tour bring with them their own interests and hopes for prompting action. So four or five people, who more often than not do not know one another beforehand, spend most of the week together and find themselves going through the same experience, each with their own preoccupations, and each taking away something different. They talk furiously all through the week, swapping impressions and trying to make connections between what they have seen and heard and their own institutions at home, and the results are always the same: commitment in one way or another by the majority to try to introduce some fresh development at home. It is always an interesting example of the power of group dynamics.

Probably an additional reason for the evident success of study tours is that every detail of the arrangements is made in advance, and the group is accompanied by someone who knows intimately the institutions to be visited, knows the administrators and faculty who will spend time with the group, and can head off lines of inquiry which are likely to prove cul-de-sacs and focus the inquiries without wasting time. So when the hosts explain what they do and how they do it, it is relatively easy to promote deeply probing discussions about some of the most sensitive aspects of their work. There has never been any question of outright adoption. It remains part of an effort to promote an appropriate version of APEL in Britain, adapting the American experience.

British participants learn a good deal about higher education in America, how the different kinds of institution fit into the overall pattern and, of particular importance these days, how they are coping with the same kinds of financial constraints experienced in Britain and how they then attempt to extend or even sustain their enrolments using all sorts of devices to increase their retention rates and make contractual deals with business and industry. In all this APEL plays a crucial role for many of them, and the hands-on experience proves time and again a valuable approach to staff development.

Increasingly there are informal APEL networks in Britain which try to provide some version of that hands-on experience. Workshops and seminars are provided in many places. Visits to colleges and universities are growing in number, but so far nothing like the systematic approach adopted for study tours to the USA has yet appeared. Ideas are gestating, however, for creating a team of academic staff who are now well versed in all the niceties of practising APEL in Britain so that on request seminars and workshops can be conducted in universities and colleges. There is plenty of scope for this kind of travelling road show as a show-case for experiential learning.

There are several different topics related to APEL which can be offered in seminars. There is the obvious topic of the current state of the art in Britain. Although there is now widespread talk about APEL it is often surprising how little people know about the range of its applications. And they are extensive. Lifting eyes from a single institution to the way, say, health and community care organizations or British Telecom have set about exploiting the possibilities offered through APEL can sometimes be something of a revelation. It can also be reassuring. What may seem like an odd idea to be handled with suspicion can become interesting when there is evidence that it is a normal idea for other reputable bodies which command respectful attention.

Then there is the theory, principles and practice of APEL. The best substitute for hands-on experience is for people to work through case studies of learning claims which have been submitted and assessed already, but doing the work for themselves so that they feel they are getting some experience. It can be helpful to look for things like the dangers of 'double counting': sometimes what may be claimed for experiential learning turns out to be a repetition of some prior certificated learning which is also being put forward for consideration. That possibility draws attention to another matter. A careful but quick scrutiny of an application form which includes space for a broad indication to be given about possible areas for claims for experiential learning can often indicate that it is not worth an individual's while attempting APEL. This may be because of the double counting issue. It may be that the individual's claim for experiential learning does not fit the award the candidate has in view. The experiential learning may be at the wrong level. Or it may be that it looks doubtful that sufficient evidence could be adduced to support the claim. Whatever the reason, it is important at the outset that the candidate has a pretty good understanding of what the chances will be for claiming credit for experiential learning. In turn that can be affected by the distinction between general and specific credit, and amounts and level of credit, all of which are affected by the structure and regulations of a particular course.

All these theoretical factors can become reality when people have documents in their hands which were prepared by actual applicants and have been assessed by academic staff. Credit accumulation and transfer is a closely related topic, as are evaluating learning outcomes and the assessment of work-based learning for academic credit. Some of the more technical aspects of data collection and record keeping can be another effective approach to a seminar for professional development.

What some people fail to recognize is that with the emergence of varied patterns of student participation, whether as full-time, part-time, periodic, occasional students as well as employment-based students, institutions have an entirely new problem of keeping exact information about when students are enrolled in any mode, for how long, what they enrol for and when they move out and then come back in again. This is a matter of huge financial significance. And APEL becomes a significant issue in trying to devise the principles on which that information is going to be collected (Dearden and Evans, 1994). Discussion of any of those topics in staff development seminars raises questions about the best approach to dealing with APEL at all. Portfolios inevitably come up, but enabling staff to handle materials which have actually gone through the APEL process makes the point forcefully that anything which provides a direct and fast route must be available for identifying and documenting claims based on experiential learning. So guidelines and student handbooks come in for discussion.

This discussion can easily introduce another range of considerations. A student needs two forms of help. The first is a general introduction to the notion of systematic reflection on experience, with examples of how to extract statements of the knowledge and skill acquired through experience and the kinds of evidence which are necessary to support any claim. A general introduction of this kind can apply to anyone setting out on the experiential learning path. The second form of help needs to be specific, to enable the student to relate possible claims for experiential learning to whatever qualification is the target and to the component parts of the course leading to that qualification. There is a problem here. Because the regulations and requirements of different courses in the same institution are likely to be different, it can well be the case that each qualification needs its own version of specific guidance for students. More than that, because courses leading to the same qualification in different institutions can have the same titles but are significantly different in structure and content, specific guidance for APEL candidates for say one Business Studies or Information Technology degree in one institution is likely to be different from another. The point of this for seminars of professional development and preparation is that it brings out the differences between disciplines in their requirements, and their criteria for assessment, all of which can put APEL in a wider context than through concentrating on its technicalities.

How this kind of professional support for staff is best provided depends on the state of APEL development in the institution in question. It needs to be sponsored from the top. There is little point in a group of relatively junior staff getting enthused about APEL unless there is support forthcoming for developments which can follow. When an institution is starting from scratch, a good start is to hold what is essentially an awareness seminar for a small group of senior staff, which should include potential supporters and known sceptics. If that leads to one or two deciding the idea is worth exploring further, then the next stage is to convene a group of academic staff drawn from interested departments or programme areas for a workshop on the procedures and practices which are the basis for successful development. If that goes down well then the next stage is to run a pilot scheme to test the waters so the institution has some evidence of its own to consider alongside all the evidence which can now be culled from outside. Interested groups of staff in other departments may want to know more about APEL. Where there is a professional development unit it can take the lead in promoting all these activities.

This approach to the professional preparation of academic staff for developing schemes for APEL rests on the classical proposition that a prophet is without honour in his own country. An outsider may be no more knowledgeable than people in the institution itself but can act as a catalyst for discussion, a lightning conductor for controversy. And that can be very useful for a topic like APEL when academic scepticism, sometimes really an expression of anxiety and uncertainty, can become vigorous, especially when questions of academic standards and assessments get a good airing. The outsider's head can be put on the block, rather than a colleague's. At the right time, too, it can be invaluable for former students who have been through the APEL procedures to contribute to a seminar.

There is another possible dimension to seminars on APEL where it relates to the assessment of work-based learning for academic credit. Any discussion of that leads into all kinds of considerations of what actually happens in the workplace, and what it is possible to learn through work. As soon as negotiated learning agreements enter the discussion the implications for students of becoming more responsible for their own learning become obvious, and thus the academic supervisor's role tends to become more closely defined. If the object of learning through work is to be realized, then that learning has to be intentional. And at that point the role of supervisors and line managers also comes into sharper focus. Staff development for academics then begins to extend to the staff development of supervisors and line managers in employment. As work-based learning for academic credit becomes more widespread, the preparation of employers who will act as mentors to students and play their part in assessment is bound to become a serious undertaking for the higher education institution. All of this relates in one way and another to helping students become more employable as well as becoming more self-reliant for their learning and so connects with the central purposes of the institution.

But perhaps the most significant aspect of APEL for staff development is the understanding that it is merely a form of learning which is being brought within the purview of academic institutions. Perhaps the time has come to stop thinking about it as something extra, but to look on it as an aspect of the assessment of learning. In other words, now that the implications of the assessment of experiential learning are taking root, its incorporation as part of an institution's mainstream commitment to students can best be served by abandoning the very words experiential learning and concentrating instead on expanding the concept of assessment to take account of all the various modes of learning which are now accepted as valid.

Another dimension to staff development becomes obvious when current experiential learning is incorporated in any form of formal certification. Usually that implies work-based learning. Earlier the case was made that work-based learning only becomes significant when it is intentional. Making work-based learning intentional requires the 'mentoring' of students by those who may be called their supervisors, either at work or from the university or college. In each case mentors need to be properly prepared to do their job. Mentoring in the sense of encouraging those for whom a mentor is responsible to learn from their work is not an entirely straightforward business (Ashworth and Sexton, 1992). Employers have to learn to add a new range of skills to those they habitually use as supervisors. Apart from anything else, they have to come to terms with the various forms of assessment that are part and parcel of making judgements about individuals' levels of knowledge and skill, which in turn are a necessary part of awarding qualifications. Academic staff have to learn the realities of the workplace before they can help their students to learn from the tasks they undertake, and similarly be prepared to develop their ideas about appropriate procedures for assessment. For both, then, some form of staff development is essential.

My emphasis on the need for adequate preparation for those who are going to be involved in assessment of experiential learning does not necessarily mean that the best approach is through formal tuition sessions. They have their part, naturally, but the best way of learning to do the job is experientially. Tackling the tasks involved with the support of an experienced colleague is the surest route to satisfactory performance.

Riding on APEL, things have gone full circle, with professional development doing its institutional job. APEL in its many aspects can serve many masters at the same time.

REFERENCES

Ashworth, Peter and Saxton, Judy (1992): *Managing Work Experience.* London: Routledge.

FURTHER READING

BTEC (1990): *The Assessment of Prior Learning: Guidelines.* London: Business and Technician Education Council.
Buckle, John (1988): *A Learner's Guide to Building on Your Experience.* London: Learning from Experience Trust.
City & Guilds (1990): *Assessment Handbook* and *APL Handbook.*
Dearden, Gerald and Evans, Norman (1994): *Curriculum Opportunity: AP(E)L in Higher Education.* London: Learning from Experience Trust.
DOE (1988–): *Competence and Assessment,* Quarterly Journal of the Employment Department's Method Strategy Unit. Various articles.
Simosko, Susan (1991): *APL: A Practical Guide for Professionals.* London: Kogan Page.

11

APEL as an International Development

One of the most interesting things about the international development of APEL is that in different countries it has been related to different kinds of issues and has been handled differently as a result. Chronologically, substantial developments occurred first in the USA, from the early 1970s, then in Great Britain and Canada, and afterwards in France, Australia and New Zealand, while growing interest is being shown in an increasing number of other countries, such as Indonesia, and enthusiasts are busy trying to whip up interest elsewhere. There are two common denominators running through these developments. The individuals who take the initiative in promoting APEL tend to believe that it offers ways of improving the service to individuals through formal and informal education and as a consequence are interested in change and institutional development. Equity is a compelling issue for them. At an entirely different level, APEL is now seen as part of a general attempt to strengthen the economy through striving to achieve a better educated and trained working population. An important difference is that whereas in the USA there has been no significant government support, and charitable trusts and foundations have encouraged and sponsored activities, in other countries government agencies have been directly involved in promoting and financing APEL initiatives.

In the USA APEL appeared on the agenda in the early 1970s when universities and colleges were recruiting larger numbers of older students as a response to social, economic and demographic change. A number of colleges had been created specially to serve the needs of these older students, deploying various forms of non-traditional learning. A powerful Carnegie Commission on Non-traditional Study was established to examine the opportunities for adults to learn in higher education. It included in its report (1973) two recommendations which related directly to experiential learning: 'New devices and techniques should be perfected to measure the outcomes of the many types of non-traditional study and to assess the educative effect of work experience and community service' and 'systems of quality control should be built into the instruction and evaluative aspects of non-traditional study wherever possible'. 'They wanted to shore up the academic currency system against abuses in awarding credit' (Gamson, 1989).

As a result of the strong support from members of the Commission, in 1974 a three-year research programme was set up by the Education Testing Service at Princeton (ETS) under the title of the Co-operative Assessment of Experiential Learning (CAEL), funded primarily by the Carnegie Corporation of New York but with additional support from the Ford Foundation, the Lilly Endowment and the Fund for the Improvement of Post-Secondary Education, a government agency.

CAEL's purpose was to evolve valid and reliable ways of making academic assessments of the knowledge and skill which people had acquired through their life, work and leisure experiences – learning gained outside the classroom – and then to publish guidelines to encourage their use in post-secondary institutions. It produced a steady flow of reports, 54 in all, on the various aspects of its work, with the *Principles of Good Practice in Assessing Experiential Learning* by Warren Willingham (published 1977) as a summary and distillation of its findings. For twelve years Willingham's pamphlet was the essential reference point for the assessment of experiential learning until Urban Whittaker produced its successor for CAEL – *Assessing Learning; Standards, Principles and Procedures* (1989). Both Willingham and Whittaker were part of the core group of people involved with CAEL from its inception.

CAEL began with nine institutions as participants and Morris Keeton, a member of ETS and Provost of Antioch College, became the chairman of the group. There was such strong interest in the project that Morris Keeton secured far wider participation than was first envisaged and by the time the three-year funding was up, some 243 institutions were involved. That was the first CAEL. They decided not to disband and constituted themselves into the second CAEL: the Council for the Advancement of Experiential Learning, with Morris as the founding Executive Director. He secured a five-year grant from the Kellogg Foundation for the Institutional Development Programme to carry forward the practice in universities and colleges and, with exemplary skill, secured funding from a variety of other bodies so that CAEL was sustained as a project-driven, soft money organization right up to 1984, ending with an annual budget of 2.6 million dollars.

In 1983 Morris Keeton commissioned Zelda Gamson to write a study of CAEL. Her preface begins, 'This is the story of an organization that set out to change a small part of higher education and ended up doing much more.' She took four years to complete the study, which was published by CAEL in association with Longwood as *Higher Education and the Real World: The Story of CAEL*. After her exhaustive investigation Zee Gamson concluded that Morris Keeton's vision for experiential learning was one of ever-improved services for adult learners. This appealed to a wide variety of educators in the USA and later abroad so that experiential learning became something of a social movement. As such its agenda was to seek ways of opening up higher education to those who either were or thought they were excluded. Experiential learning could be a catalyst for institutional change and reform.

That was the essential point of the Institutional Development Programme of CAEL 2. The programme included an ambitious professional staff training element in the theory and practice of the assessment of prior and sponsored (current) experiential learning. It was followed by a variety of other approaches, such as a freephone call-line giving advice to potential students about where they could find experiential learning programmes to suit them; early attempts to put all that information on an interactive computer system; a study leading to a categorization of institutional practices identified as conditions conducive for adults to succeed in higher education, and the publication of a 20-volume Jossey-Bass series, New Directions for Experiential Learning.

Despite this remarkable succession of initiatives, despite the powerful, consistent, enthusiastic support of many institutions and countless hundreds of individuals, and despite Morris Keeton's reputation as an outstanding leader in higher education, by 1988, as Zee Gamson noted, CAEL's impact on higher education as a whole was slight. There were many reasons for that. Traditional academics and academic institutions do not take readily to innovations suggested from outside. The structure of many higher education institutions placed Continuing Education for Adults on the periphery, and since experiential learning was most likely to be deployed for adult learners through Continuing Education it too tended to be marginal. The separation of administrators from academic staff also meant that administrators running Continuing Education often had difficulty in securing the collaboration of teaching faculty as assessors for experiential learning. Given such circumstances, when someone responsible for an experiential learning programme left, the programme could easily lapse. Thus there were many reasons why experiential learning and its assessment did not gain much ground in universities and colleges, outside the 300–400 which were members of CAEL.

There may well have been a different reason; assessment by portfolio. From the time of the Carnegie Commission onwards it was established that there were a variety of ways of assessing prior and experiential learning. There were two programmes of external examinations, one as the College Level Examination Programme and one as the American College Testing programme. These are examinations, set on prescribed syllabuses open to anyone who registers, and are approved for academic credit towards either an associate or baccalaureate degree, provided, that is, that the university or college in question accepts those results for credit. The American military has a vast range of tests and examinations, some of which are approved for academic credit with the same proviso. Many companies have had some of their in-house courses of education and training rated for academic credit. Both the military's and the companies' courses are listed in publications issued by the American Council on Education with brief syllabus descriptions and the credits recommended both for amount and level. Some institutions offer challenge examinations of their own devising with the same intention. All of these are devices for enabling individuals to have their off-campus learning assessed for academic credit. So they are all approaches to the assessment of experiential learning.

From the outset CAEL set particular importance on what

came to be called comprehensive individualized portfolio-assisted assessment. This described a process whereby individuals were enabled to review their past experience, identify occasions when they thought they had learned something, record what they had learned, and then produce evidence to support the claim they were making. Psychologically this was an exceptionally powerful approach for adults returning to learning. It enabled them to take stock of themselves, recognize for themselves what they had achieved as learners without recourse to academic institutions, get a good sense of what they wanted to learn in the future, all of which was highly motivating. To support this approach CAEL published handbooks on portfolio development, and on assessment of experiential learning produced in portfolios. This was the most substantial part of the staff development programme. For CAEL, therefore, individualized and portfolio-assisted assessment was a central issue. It was and is all of a piece with the overriding interest in improving the service for adult learners. It fits the idea of CAEL representing something of a social as well as education movement.

However, it was also a highly charged academic issue. At one level it brought into the open the potential significance of learning acquired without any reference to academic staff. At a quite different level it required academics, as professionals, to undertake academic assessments based on unfamiliar forms of evidence without any of the customary tools to guide them. At a different level again, reading through portfolios, which could be voluminous, represented a lengthy task and not one necessarily to the liking of many academics. And of course somehow there had to be a fee structure which could accommodate these activities, with the additional complications of compensation for academic staff who acted as assessors.

It could well be, therefore, that the factors associated with portfolio assessment contributed to the resistance to incorporate APEL in the regular mainstream activities of some universities and colleges.

All that is at an institutional level. There are also two supra-institutional factors which help to explain the relatively slow adoption of APEL by many American higher education institutions: the role of the federal and state governments in education and the absence of an external body with executive authority for academic affairs. Neither of these factors affects the experience of Great Britain, Canada, Australia or New Zealand.

The federal government has little if any direct influence, let alone control, over the academic provision of higher education. Thus it is difficult to talk of a national system. Until comparatively recently, state governments were more or less sleeping partners in state-funded higher education. Under current budgetary problems they have become wide-awake partners, worrying about value for money, and some have intervened directly in higher education to the extent of putting a moratorium on experiential learning programmes as state-funded activities. But the key point in relation to the spread of experiential learning activities is that apart from in one or two states, such as California and Florida, there has been no direct lead from state government or its agencies for the adoption of experiential learning programmes.

The second supra-institutional factor is that there never has been in the USA an academic body like the Council for National Academic Awards in Britain. There are the eight Regional Accrediting Associations but they are voluntary and are not executive in the same way as the former CNAA. As shown in previous chapters, in Britain once CNAA had ruled that experiential learning was eligible for academic credit at both bachelor's and master's levels, half the higher education provision in the land had been given both a licence and a lead to develop schemes for APEL. And since a government minister for higher education extolled the virtues of doing just that at a public press launch for the Credit and Accumulation Registry of CNAA, the lead was strong. No such national conduit for influencing higher education exists in the USA, and that too underlay the difficulties CAEL experienced in trying to influence higher education directly.

However, the direct attempt to get institutions to change their ways and, despite them if necessary, improve opportunities for adults to learn, is only the first part of the American story; part two is about an indirect approach to the same objective that was provided fortuitously by industry. Here is another important contrast between developments of APEL in the USA and the rest of the world. It is a cultural difference. There is a stronger belief in the USA than in many other countries that studying and gaining additional qualifications should be part of being an adult. There is a concomitant willingness by employers to accept that employees who learn are better employees than those who do not, and to spend money on supporting learning.

Just at the time when Morris Keeton was finding resistance to providing funding for new projects, CAEL got involved as an academic adviser and then broker for the College and Universities Option Programme within the Ford Motor Company/ United Automobile Workers jointly-sponsored Employee Development Programme. Basically, CAEL was employed to devise ways of interesting Ford workers to return to some form of additional learning, to arrange facilities for the assessment of prior and experiential learning, to line up colleges and universities willing and able to accept Ford workers as students. That was in 1986. From that beginning CAEL now has some twenty contracts, all over the United States, each offering some variation on the Ford/UAW scheme.

Those developments have been critical for the progress of CAEL. Through industry and commerce a route opened up for serving the very learners CAEL was most concerned about. Since the success of any Employee Development Scheme implied getting universities and colleges to provide what an EDP wanted, which was not necessarily what they were in the habit of offering, there was an indirect way of influencing what institutions actually did. CAEL strongly encouraged colleges and institutions to develop APEL schemes and also advised workers which institutions were able to offer those facilities. Any institution choosing not to offer APEL schemes would forfeit the opportunity of attracting additional fee-paying students. For CAEL the contracts provided a source of earned income to replace the decling amounts of money coming for special projects – though that in turn meant a huge increase in CAEL staff, with all the institutional problems linked to larger size.

The position now is that in the USA Employee Development Programmes which incorporate experiential learning are seen increasingly as a vital contribution to the upskilling of the workforce. And because that is taken seriously by politicians, CAEL is now promoting APEL as a matter of public policy at state and federal levels. So APEL in the USA shows both the strengths and weaknesses of voluntary non-statutory initiatives.

If that is an American story, it is a story from which other countries have learned and gained inspiration. Every country which has developed schemes of APEL bears some of the marks of influence from part one of the American story, however far they may diverge from American practice. Unfortunately, the lessons from part two of the story still have to be learned.

As shown in previous chapters, the developments in Britain have gone through an initial voluntary phase, assisted powerfully by the Council for National Academic Awards and the Further Education Unit, both of which funded pilot projects using public money, followed by heavy encouragement from the government's Employment Department (not the Department for Education, be it noted) using two approaches. The first was supporting voluntary education, through funding specific projects in post-secondary education through its Training, Education and Enterprise Division. The second came through supporting courses related to the National Council for Vocational Qualifications, which while they are strictly voluntary have gained a quasi-statutory status because of the way funding formulae for further education colleges are being increasingly related to vocational qualifications.

In Canada things were entirely different. It began in Quebec. There, in 1982, a Study Commission on Adult Education recommended that the Quebec government should implement Prior Learning Assessment through the education system to help returning adults to obtain qualifications. This was followed, two years later, by a policy statement about a) implementing PLA through the education system, b) amending regulations so that from 1984 students could get academic credit for their non-academic learning, and c) financing a development programme backed by government departments and the institutions themselves. CAEL was commissioned to assist with a two-year training programme to prepare staff in the institutions to undertake the work (Isabelle and Landry, 1988).

In the late 1980s British Columbia began a distance learning initiative to provide APEL facilities throughout the Province, where much of the thinly scattered population had no easy access to universities or colleges. Since 1979 the Open College and Open University had offered open learning courses. But in 1988 the Province set up the British Columbia Educational Credit Bank as a central institution. APEL kits were specially designed for the purpose, again with consultancy help from CAEL, to take students through all the various stages: reflection; writing competence statements; plotting their future pathways of study and learning. These kits were made available to individual students who were then linked for tutorial purposes with staff in regional institutions, by phone line or electronic mail facilities if necessary. Through the Credit Bank individuals were enabled to enter either the college or university track of institutions.

In Ontario things developed differently again. An official report published in July 1992, *Prior Learning Assessment: Enhancing the Access of Adult Learners to Ontario's Colleges*, began: 'In the summer of 1991, the Minister of Colleges and Universities, Richard Allen, asked the Council of Regents, a policy and planning advisory body to the Minister, to establish an Advisory Committee to advise him on the development and implementation of a system of prior learning assessment (PLAS) for Ontario's colleges.' The introduction goes on to say that in April that year 2,300 copies of its discussion document went out to 23 colleges and 263 external agencies. So when the Minister issued the Advisory Committee's final report in October 1992, saying, 'I believe PAL is an important initiative which will improve access in post-secondary education in Ontario', he did so from solid evidence. At the time of writing, the introduction of a system-wide approach in Ontario waits on a cabinet decision.

Thus for Canada APEL has come as a series of top-down developments, some of which were statutory requirements and others being urged on powerfully by education authorities backed by public funding.

France is different again. There APEL developments are quite separate from the education system, except that a decree authorized the use of APEL for entry to higher education where candidates did not have a baccalaureate. A government edict established 70 Centres de Bilan throughout the country, where individuals up to top technician level can go for what is essentially an APEL assessment, a kind of personal audit of skills and knowledge. The idea is that they can then make better judgements about what kind of job to seek in employment, or about their own career development. The system was set up to help cope with the crisis in employment, concern about transferable skills and the problems of technological transformation. It is all at a technician level. It has nothing to do with accreditation.

Australian interest in APEL grew from a number of personal inquiries from individuals to the Learning from Experience Trust in Britain and CAEL in the USA during a period of rapid change and development in higher education as a whole, when increased participation was posing problems not least because of the anticipated increase in the numbers of older students. Fundamentally these developments in Australia are part and parcel of an overall thrust to increase the economic strength of the country.

In New Zealand things are different again. There APEL is part of a thoroughgoing reorganization of the educational system undertaken by the government, also with an eye to strengthening the country's ability to cope with the emerging developments in the global economy. A New Zealand Qualifications Authority has been set up with a brief to fulfil the legislative requirements of including PLA (as they refer to APEL) in the National Qualifications Framework. It is busy promoting PLA activities through research projects, conferences and seminars and consultative documents, drawing on some of the experience in the USA and UK through contacts with both CAEL and the Learning from Experience Trust.

The National Qualifications Framework is composed of eight levels, in which level 1 is roughly comparable to the fifth year of secondary schooling and level 7 is comparable to the final stage of a three-year diploma or first degree. PLA can be used at all levels. Private tutors are required to register with the NZQA, and government training establishments need to obtain its recognition as a quality assurance measure and to become eligible for receiving government funds. Accreditation by the NZQA authorizes a provider to deliver nationally recognized courses, and this stands as a second quality measure.

However, this top-down approach stops short of telling institutions how to conduct PLA procedures through setting out models. Guidelines were provided but institutions were left to work out their own ways of tackling PLA, always with the proviso that everything will be audited by the NZQA.

In Indonesia the picture is different again, though with the same underlying economic thrust. And again CAEL has been instrumental in introducing to that country the possibilities offered by APEL. An Indonesian professor of education who attended a CAEL conference made connections between APEL and the problems facing his country in upgrading the qualifications of teachers and increasing their numbers. CAEL was invited to provide a six-day workshop for 25 Indonesian participants drawn from ten different training establishments to learn about experiential learning theory, standards for assessing experiential learning and practices for portfolio development and assessment. It was all new for them and meant switching from time-based courses to assessing learning. As one participant put it, 'To know what a person has learned we [are used to looking] for the seal on his papers.' But the same influences were at work as elsewhere: a multiplicity of learning opportunities outside the formal education structure. Implementation depended on the participants getting approval for their APEL proposals from their faculty and administrative colleagues. There are signs that APEL may be sponsored by the Ministry of Education and Culture and that activities may spread out from teacher training to other parts of higher education.

The most recent indication of the appeal and utility of APEL comes from South Africa. In the wake of the elections which saw Nelson Mandela become President, initiatives with the Ford Foundation are being pursued in earnest with likely cooperation from CAEL in the USA and LET in the UK. The motives are similar to those elsewhere; social concern and economic necessity.

What this brief account of international development in APEL shows is that from the seed bed of the USA a whole range of different shoots have grown. Each shoot has been fertilized by the general proposition that learning acquired without reference to formal education institutions merits close attention by those formal institutions. Doing so is a sensible response to the rapidly changing economic and social circumstances in which individuals are now living. National worries about demography and economies are intensified by the international dimensions to both those national factors. So it is hardly surprising that APEL is of acute interest internationally.

REFERENCES

Gamson, Zelda F. (1989): *Higher Education and the Real World: The Story of CAEL*. Chicago: Longwood/CAEL.

Isabelle, Robert and Landry, Francis (1988). In Simosko, Susan et al., *Assessing Learning*. Chicago: CAEL.

FURTHER READING ON THE USA

Chickering, Arthur et al. (1981): *The Modern American College*. San Francisco: Jossey-Bass.
Evans, Norman (1981): *The Knowledge Revolution*. London: Grant McIntyre.
Evans, Norman (1985): *Post Education Society*. Beckenham: Croom Helm.
Evans, Norman (1992): *Experiential Learning: Assessment and Accreditation*. London: Routledge.
Keeton, M. T. et al. (1976): *Experiential Learning: Rationale, Characteristics and Assessment*. San Francisco: Jossey-Bass.
Whittaker, Urban (1989): *Assessing Learning; Standards, Principles and Procedures*. Chicago: CAEL.
Willingham, Warren (1977): *Principles of Good Practice in Assessing Experiential Learning*. Columbia: CAEL.

FURTHER READING ON VARIOUS COUNTRIES

Weil, Susan and McGill, Ian (eds) (1989): *Making Sense of Experiential Learning*. Milton Keynes: SRHE/Open University Press.

12

APEL for the Future

Experiential learning offers opportunities to individuals to experience success as learners through enabling them to realize what they have learned without knowing they have learned it. As such it is a positive contribution towards achieving the learning society without which the country's economic prospects are bleak.

At an institutional level experiential learning is saying that learning takes place in many different places, and that sometimes what is learned outside formal education can be as valuable as, sometimes more valuable than, what is learned directly from formal tuition. That is now accepted as a factual statement. As such it represents a significant change in attitudes towards learning and therefore towards teaching. That change of attitude is being expressed in policies coming from government departments, and in practice throughout the education world and in employment and training.

At a national level, therefore, experiential learning can shine a bright encouraging light, if only there is the imagination to use it. The employed, the unemployed, offenders young and old, the professions, the education institutions themselves, all have much to gain wherever its possibilities are exploited.

The importance of that change in attitude to experiential learning is that it is simply one aspect of change in modern technological societies. Many other changes are taking place, affecting the population as a whole with consequences for learning which are as profound as those that APEL represents. APEL is one piece of a mosaic.

Take the most important factor for any household: the relationship between life at home and life at work. Familiar patterns are fast disappearing. As well as nuclear families, there are evolving patterns of single-parent households and extended families. As full-time employment becomes less and less the norm for millions of people, part-time work, job sharing, fixed-term contracts for people at all levels, home-stay work, oscillations between employment and unemployment, returning to learning and training to cope with career change, all are producing entirely different patterns of domestic life. And with those different patterns go changing patterns of learning and assumptions about how lives are going to be lived.

Nor is that all. Demography and the economy are fast changing the very structures of society. Government's reaction to these changes is changing the relationship between individuals and the state as indirect taxation increases in proportion to direct taxation. The relationship between elected members of Parliament and their constituents is changed, and Parliament itself has a different relationship with government as the executive acquires more and more centralized power. And all of this is made more complicated by membership of, and the influences stemming from, the European Union.

The European Union can easily pose problems for APEL because Continental countries have not generally developed APEL procedures and applications in the same way as in Britain. When APEL contributes to nationally recognized academic, vocational or professional awards, there may well be difficulties in getting those qualifications recognized in partner countries. That conflict between freedom of movement for persons and freedom of recognition of qualifications and so employment will not be resolved easily.

That is the context for thinking about APEL in the future. Lifelong learning becomes an essential for economic survival. It also becomes an essential condition for individual survival. So what people can learn, how they learn it, and what use they can make of it is deadly serious. And as these changes work their way through society there will be more and more ways of people learning.

The need for the accreditation of learning and for qualifications is bound to continue, however regrettable that development may seem to some people. But as the modes of learning expand,

and more people make more use of the opportunities offered for learning electronically, for example, so will ways of accrediting learning need to expand. Informal ways of learning are likely to become systems in their own right. And to the extent that informally acquired learning can be seen as prior and experiential, its assessment is an issue for individuals, educators, employers and government alike.

The moves in many institutions to establish a scheme for credit accumulation, thus creating ladders of opportunities for people to work towards gaining qualifications, underlines the need for developments of that kind. So do attempts to go beyond that and devise policies to establish a national framework for credit accumulation running through all post-secondary education provision. The Further Education Unit's consultative document *A Basis for Credit* produced a series of suggestions. The National Credit Accumulation and Transfer project of the Higher Education Quality Council, funded jointly by the Department for Education and the Employment Department, is currently exploring those very questions.

In that context student-paced and student-centred learning take on new and urgent meanings within credit accumulation arrangements. So does portable academic credit, which allows men and women to undertake study in one institution and transfer achievements/credits to another at will. It is all to do with keeping open the widest range of learning opportunities; access in the widest interpretation. It is vital within the United Kingdom, but given developments in the European Union, despite the potential short-term difficulties, it is likely to become important for increasing numbers of people.

Given the way that APEL has acted and can continue to act as a catalyst for those developments, it is a fundamental part of the move towards a learning society. For education that means moving APEL to centre stage. It also means moving other forms of learning, such as open learning systems, distance learning and interactive computer-assisted learning to centre stage. All those opportunities for learning have been introduced piecemeal, erratically, and usually at the periphery. They tend to be provided and offered by enthusiasts. In only a few universities and colleges have such forms of learning been assimilated fully as mainstream provision for education.

And this is the central challenge posed by APEL for education. It is for formal educational institutions to reorganize the way they set about their work so as to take full account of all the ways of learning which now exist. A college or university needs to become a Learning Centre where classroom teaching is seen as only one opportunity offered to individual students. Like computer-assisted learning or work-based learning, experiential learning then becomes merely a different mode of learning which suits some people, but not others, and finds its proper place in the battery of assessment procedures devised to enable institutions to make public statements about the quality of the qualifications and awards they make.

APEL now needs to stop being something slightly odd and separate from 'proper' learning. It is proper learning in its own right. Perhaps the very label should be abandoned. That label has served its purpose.

The same challenge is posed for employers. There is much talk about human capital being the best resource for companies. To make the best use of that best resource employers need to know what it is, and on the whole they do not know. APEL can offer ways of enabling them to know. By analogy with education, the assessment of experiential learning needs to become an integral part of a company's personnel and training policies. As for education, that implies a radical reorganization.

APEL may be a commonsense, simple proposition. When it is applied to higher education, further education, adult education, vocational and professional education or employment, public or private, it shakes the structure. It is part of the future.

Index